The Mother

Adilakshmi

Printed in Germany

Mother Meera
Oberdorf 4a
65599 Dornburg-Thalheim
Germany
Tel: +49-6436-2305
Fax: +49-6436-2361

First edition published in 1987 in Germany
Second edition published in 1994 in Germany
Third edition published in 1995 in Germany

Contents

Who is Mother Meera?

She is the living Incarnation of the Divine Mother.

What is an Incarnation?

An incarnation is the Divine in human form come on earth to help humanity to know and realize the Divine.

What is the difference between Mother Meera and the Divine Mother?

Their Will is identical and their Consciousness is One. There is no difference.

What is the Divine Mother and what is Her work?

The Divine Mother is the Force and Consciousness that sustains Creation. She is worshipped under many names and in many cultures and She has been worshipped throughout history in many forms. But behind every form and every name, She is One, Eternal and Omnipotent. She is Transcendent and stands above all Her creations in the silence of the Absolute; She is the breath and power of all creation; She is in every part of creation forever.

The work of the Divine Mother is the transformation of humanity into God, of time into Eternity, of matter into Divine Matter. Her work is a work of transformation, and it has no end.

What is Mother Meera's work?

Mother Meera's Will and Power are the Will and Power of the Divine Mother. Mother Meera's Work and the Work of the Divine Mother are the same Work. Mother Meera has come to purify the consciousness of the earth so it may be ready for Transformation. She is calling down onto the earth the Light of the Supreme that makes Transformation certain. Her work in our time is to open all people to the power and radiance of this Light so the Divine Will may be done and the Divine Life established on earth.

Thalheim, Germany 1993

HOMAGE TO MR. REDDY

(The Bulletin of the "MOTHER MEERA SOCIETY", Canada)

From Adilakshmi we have heard with resignation about the departure of Mr. Reddy. Balgur Venkat Reddy left his body on June 20, 1985. His body was laid to rest on June 24.

When we think about Mr. Reddy, the words which spring into our mind are love, devotion, and service for the Divine Mother. Each time when we were able to meet Mr. Reddy or speak to him, we could always feel the profound devotion which this great soul had for the Mother. When he was translating or explaining the answers which Mother Meera gave us, we heard words which permitted our mind to understand, but we always perceived an invisible language which spoke to our heart and permitted us to understand in depth the meaning of Mother's answers. His words opened our hearts to the Mother. During the semi-private encounters, we were able to see and be touched on the subtle planes by the real love, the submission to the Mother, and the profound devotion which united Mr. Reddy to the Divine Mother. We perceived Mr. Reddy as a friend, a brother... and we remember the sadness which invaded us at the moment we heard about his departure. We who have seen him only for a few instants, we can only imperfectly imagine the state of the German disciples who saw him every day, the soul state of Adilakshmi who worked with him since 1974 in the service of Mother, and the Mother who looked after him in such a constant and touching manner.

We have the conviction that Mr. Reddy had found constant refuge in the consciousness of the Mother, that he was totally carried by Her, that the promise of the Gita – as commented on by Sri Aurobindo – was held:

"...I am here next to you on your war chariot, Master revealed in existence in you and outside of you, and I reiterate the formal assurance, the infallible promise to lead you to Me through and beyond any pain and any evil. Whatever the difficulties and the complexities which arise, be sure that I am leading you to a complete Divine Life in the universal Spirit and to an immortal existence in the transcendent Spirit..."

Sri Aurobindo, *Essays on the Gita*

I am all that has ever been,
I am all that is,
I am all that ever shall be,
yet never have mortal eyes
perceived me as I am.

Song to
the Mother Goddess Neit
(Egyptian)

MOTHER MEERA:
HER LIFE AND HER EXPERIENCES

Mother Meera was born Kamala Reddy, daughter of farmer parents in the village of Chandepalle, Andhra Pradesh, India, on December 26, 1960. Her parents treated Her as an exceptional child and loved Her very much. Her family was not especially religious and She was not brought up in any tradition. Her real parents were the spiritual guides that She met in vision; it was from them that She received the love and help She needed.

Her spiritual evolution was rapid and complete. Mother had no human guru, read no religious philosophy, did no sadhana, followed no special discipline; Her contact with the Absolute was immediate and unmediated. At the age of two or three She would go to 'Different Lights' when She was in need of comfort. At six She had Her first experience of Samadhi when She fell senseless for a whole day, an experience which, She tells us, taught Her complete detachment from human relations.

"From then on I knew myself to live only in the Divine and by the Divine's will and help."

Such a detachment is usually the crown of a lifetime's prayer and effort. Mother knew it at six.

Already at the age of eight Mother came to Mr. Reddy's family. At this time, Mr. Reddy was living in the Sri Aurobindo Ashram in Pondicherry and it wasn't until his uncle died in 1972 that he went back to his village to manage his property. There he found Kamala Reddy in his house. Mr. Reddy was immediately struck by Her and watching Her closely and living in Her presence convinced him that She was exceptional.

"My first experience of Her power happened like this... Mother Meera had gone to stay fifty miles away. I was lying on my bed one evening. I heard Her voice calling me and was amazed. How could She come all that way? I got up and looked for Her. I could not find Her anywhere. Later I went to the city where She was. She said to me, 'I came to you and you did not notice anything. I called out to you and you didn't hear.' I asked Her how She had come that far. She just said that there was 'another way of travelling'."

In 1974, Mr. Reddy decided to take Meera to the Ashram in Pondicherry. Mother's first visit to the samadhi of Sri Aurobindo and Sweet Mother resulted in the following experience, related in Her own words to Mr. Reddy, who has preserved an exact record of this as of other experiences. Mother Meera was fourteen years old.

* * *

I went to the Samadhi. I did Pranam. And then I saw clearly how the bodies of Sweet Mother and Sri Aurobindo were laid in the tomb. I saw Sri Aurobindo as a young boy surrounded by members of his family. And then I saw Sweet Mother and Sri Aurobindo waking up, as if from a trance. Sweet Mother walked to a chair under a tree in the Ashram and sat down. I ran to Her. Sweet Mother caressed me, took me into Her Lap, and blessed me. She handed me the flower "Prosperity".

When I left Sweet Mother, the big hooded serpent Nagendra came up to me, blocked my way, and asked me to give up the flower. I was not frightened, but I didn't know what to do. Finally I decided to give him the flower and went back to Sweet Mother to tell Her what had happened. Meanwhile Nagendra had coiled around Sri Aurobindo and Sweet Mother's feet. Nagendra left them, ran towards me and said, "So you want to tell Sri Aurobindo and Sweet Mother what I did to you! I'll give you another white prosperity flower instead. Take it." He and I became friends then and talked together. While he talked I suddenly felt he was hungry. At once a cow appeared. Its udders were bulging with milk. I picked up a pot and milked the cow and gave the milk to Nagendra. Then he went off to a snake pit to rest.

After a while Nagendra returned with two snake friends. With great love he spread his hood over my head while the two other snakes coiled around each of my arms. The snakes stayed with me, sleeping by my side, for three days.

Even while the snakes were with me, Sweet Mother and Sri Aurobindo used to take me out on expeditions. They showed me the different worlds. I asked them to stay with me instead of the snakes and they agreed very happily. And from that time I could travel to many strange places. I was taken to the depths of the sea and told their secrets. I travelled in space and felt and lived the mysteries of the Sun and Moon and the stars.

* * *

This experience was followed in the next six months by many others. "In those days," Mr. Reddy recalls, "She used to tell me almost everything. Every day She would tell me what She had seen and done on the higher planes." Here are some experiences of that time:

* * *

Once I asked Sri Aurobindo to show me "Soul Land". He agreed. After a long journey, Sri Aurobindo felt tired. We rested and then went on. After a while, we came back and I was very happy with everything that I had seen. But I couldn't speak about it. When I got back I looked at the clock and I wondered why the hands were in the same position as they had been when we started. Sri Aurobindo said that our journey was not bound by time; it had taken place in the Infinite, beyond time or space.

* * *

Once I asked Durga and Saraswati to take me with them and show me other worlds. They did and we lived together happily.

* * *

I went out with Sri Aurobindo and Sweet Mother whenever they took evening or morning walks. On one of these walks they took me with them as usual but I suddenly found myself alone. I walked on and came to a huge fort. It had a huge gateway. I was curious and I went in and found myself in a hall. There was an assembly there of yellow-bodied people wearing crowns and seated on big chairs. I was surprised. They stood up and began to pay me their respects. And then I saw that the throne in the middle was empty. I was led up to it and asked to sit on it. I agreed. I asked them all to sit too. And then I realized that they were Gods and Goddesses and that this was the hall of Gods.

After a while, I came back to earth with Sweet Mother and Sri Aurobindo.

* * *

I travelled with Sweet Mother constantly in all the worlds and I saw many beautiful things and beautiful places. But I also saw terrible and frightening things, worlds where the worst forces are at work. I asked Sweet Mother, "Why are you showing these things when you know I hate them?" Mother said, "Your work is not just in beautiful places, you are to transform darkness into light, suffering into joy and death into life."

* * *

Once Sweet Mother gave me a rose. I took the flower to Sri Aurobindo's Samadhi. I knew it was not an ordinary flower. It was my soul. I held onto it fiercely. But as I was walking, Sri Aurobindo snatched it from me without my knowing.

I was very sad because I had lost my soul. Then Sri Aurobindo called me and asked me why I was so sad. I told him that I had lost my soul. He said, "Your soul is not lost and could never be," and then he showed me the flower he had stolen. Then he replaced Sweet Mother's rose with a golden rose and told me that this golden rose was his soul and that it would stay with me always. And then he blessed me. I merged in Sweet Mother and Sweet Mother merged in me. I was told by Sweet Mother that I must look after the affairs of the whole world, that I must bear very heavy responsibilities and work unceasingly for the Divine.

* * *

Mother is still fourteen years old and yet, as these experiences make clear, it is to Her that work of transforming the world begun by Sri Aurobindo and Sweet Mother has been entrusted. It is not only Sweet Mother and Sri Aurobindo that are helping Her; all the Divine Beings come to pay Her homage and join with Her to help Her.

I must look after the affairs of the world... I must bear very heavy responsibilities and work unceasingly for the Divine.

India 1979

Mr. Reddy decided, after some months in Pondicherry, to take Meera back to Hyderabad and put Her at his own expense into a Girl's hostel. In Mr. Reddy's words, "I was now certain of Her great spiritual destiny – but I felt She should be educated. She did not want to study. It is as if She has no need of the mental plane at all, although She is, in practical life, very quick-witted. Mother's work is done above and beyond all mental constructions."

Mother spent two years at the hostel and earned the respect of everyone. The Superintendent was fond of Her and the other girls in awe of Her knowledge, withdrawn power and Her silence. It was during this time that Mother had Her Darshan of the Paramatman Light, the Light of the Supreme Lord. She has seen Lights of all kinds during Her childhood and the recent period in Pondicherry; but it was in the hostel itself that She had Her complete experience of the Paramatman. As Mother described it on February 6, 1979, five years later:

* * *

In December 1974, I was not in good health for ten days. I did not know what to do. Then I slept and heard a voice, "Ask for the darshan of Paramatman." I did not know that Paramatman was the Supreme Lord, but my heart drove me on and a Mother appeared to me and asked me, "Where are you going?" "Mother," I answered, "I heard a voice and I am going to Paramatman." The Mother didn't say anything.

At dawn I woke up. I was not well. I slept again from 7 p.m. till midnight. My whole body was shaking with pain and fear.

After twelve I heard a loud voice. It was as loud as thunder. It was as loud as if it were being made by thousands of people. When I woke up I saw I was alone and said to Paramatman, "Paramatman, I don't know who you are and I have never even heard your name. Don't trouble me like this because if I stay in this condition I'll die in a few days. I can't bear the pain and suffering. I'll wait and see if the pain returns tonight."

After 6 a.m. I saw Paramatman's dazzling Light. At 8 a.m. I woke up and my body felt much better. After this experience I know why my body became weak and tired. It was because it knew that Paramatman's Light was going to enter in. That is why I now look after it very carefully.

* * *

It became obvious that formal education would not be of any use to Mother, so Mr. Reddy took Her back to his house at the end of 1975. "When She was with me at this time She would often go into Samadhi, sometimes for fourteen hours without a break. She would sleep and eat very little. Eventually She would learn to be in trance continually, which She is, with open eyes, and able to do anything which needs doing. She was very fragile at that time and so I didn't invite or encourage anyone to see Her. I felt She needed to be alone with Her work. I knew that only solitude would allow Her development to proceed peacefully. Some villagers did come and worship Her. When She was in trance, they would just come and sit with Her and worship Her and go away when She came out of the trance. But no one was informed, no one was told anything. I didn't leave Mother for a second at that time. Durga advised me through Mother not to leave Her alone and I didn't. Even at this time when Mother was having so many and such profound experiences I did not talk philosophy or read the Gita to Her or anything. Actually She just wasn't interested. She would cut me short if I started. It is as if all our mental constructions mean nothing to Her. Her education is absolute; She has had Gods and Avatars for Her teachers; She has learnt from a fiery and immediate awareness of the soul and the Supermind everything that She has needed to know."

Here are Mother's accounts of some of the experiences of that time, as told to Mr. Reddy.

* * *

I was invited to Devaloka, where the Gods live, for an assembly of Gods and Goddesses. Durga came to me and said, "I will give you anything," and asked me what I wanted. "Do you want happiness, enjoyment and prosperity on earth or do you want to rule over the higher worlds of Gods and Goddesses?" I replied, "I don't want to rule the Gods, I want darkness to change into Light, I want the whole earth to be made Divine." Durga said, "You will have to face ugly fiends, dark forces, devils, terrible monsters, and evil spirits. You will have to bear innumerable sufferings and agonies." I said, "I have made up my mind!" Durga was very happy. She merged into me.

* * *

Other mergers into the Divine also happened at that time, during 1976. Mahakali, Mahasaraswati, Mahalakshmi merged into me. Many other Gods came and helped me, too. And blessed me. At that time I was helped by Sweet Mother and Sri Aurobindo, Krishna, Ishwara, Brahma, Vishnu, Maheshwara, and Durga, of course. And I was visited and blessed by many Gods, Saints, Ascetics, and Rishis.

* * *

It was at this time, 1976, that Mother also received many powers and blessings from the Divine Beings.

* * *

Durga called an assembly; Gods and Goddesses, Rishis and Yogis were invited. Durga asked me to receive special Powers from the Gods and Goddesses who were ready to confer their Gifts on me. I received them happily and offered them to Durga. Durga then led Adishakti forward and told me to offer the gifts to her. As soon as Adishakti touched them, they shone brilliantly and became one. She then blessed me and gave this shining unity to me. Inside it I saw Adishakti, Durga, Lakshmi, Saraswati, Parvati and all the worlds, all human beings and the whole universe. I handed over the gift to Durga. But Durga said: "It is you who need it, Meera, and that is why you received it." So I took it back and gave it to Sweet Mother, who returned it with Her blessings saying, "You keep it. It has been given to you for a purpose." I asked Mother to look after it and give it to me when I needed it. Then the assembly ended.

* * *

One day Durga gave me a dish with turmeric and vermilion in it. She told me to go to a wood nearby; but didn't tell me where I should keep the dish or whom I should give it to. I wandered over hills and down valleys and through vast frightening jungles and I lost my way. I was exhausted and disgusted. I threw the dish at a tree and sat down. The turmeric and the vermilion went all over Nagendra, the big snake, who was resting under the tree. He came up to me and showered heaps of gems over me: diamonds and sapphires, moonstones and rubies and emeralds and gold. He begged me to accept them and I did.

* * *

At this time, Vivekananda visited me and revealed to me the secrets of yoga. I also met Ramakrishna. Once Yogi Vemana (a great saint of Andhra Pradesh) also visited me. We both started to go towards the sky. Suddenly we stopped growing; we had reached a roof. A voice said, "This roof was made by Gods. You cannot grow beyond it." I stared at the roof fiercely. Some holes were bored into it, from which different coloured lights descended.

I still wasn't satisfied. I really wanted to demolish the roof altogether. I looked at it again, even more fiercely. The roof dissolved and light poured down in an unbroken stream. We went on growing and growing. When we had reached another level, we heard another voice saying, "If you want the supramental manifestations, you must stop here. Otherwise you can carry on!" I decided that what I wanted most was the transformation of the earth, the manifestation of the Supramental on earth, and so stopped.

* * *

I was invited by Yamaraj to visit the lower worlds. Yamaraj, the god of death, showed me all living beings, from the smallest to the largest, the lowest to the highest, distributed in several series on several levels. I understood all the laws and principles of that world, especially the process of Evolution.

* * *

Once I was fighting against all the dark forces of the universe. Krishna handed me a sceptre that would give me complete success. I accepted it. It merged into me. The evil forces were completely defeated.

* * *

I went on a journey alone to a distant mountain. Sri Aurobindo tried to dissuade me, since the mountain was dangerous and no one had dared to climb it. I still went, the cliffs were vertical and slippery. It was very hard to climb them, but I got to the top. There was a cow there who came running to me as if it had been looking for me for a long time. Milk was oozing from its udder. It came up to me to be caressed and asked me to milk it and drink its milk. Meanwhile Sri Aurobindo, who had been worried about me, followed me, exhausted. I didn't know what to do with the vast amount of milk still flowing from the cow's udder: Sri Aurobindo told me that I should give Nagendra one teat to suck, I myself should drink from the second teat, Sri Aurobindo himself would drink from the third, Sweet Mother from the fourth (the other half of the udder being reserved for Saraswati). Daily we used to come back to this place, at a fixed time, and drink as much as we wanted of the milk.

* * *

One day under a tree I could see whoever I thought of and could get what I wanted. Gods and Goddesses appeared before me. From that time on I was able to use my powers, and achieve whatever I wanted or needed.

* * *

Once at this time I identified with an avadhuta who had reached the state of Nirguna Parabrahman. I experienced it fully also. The condition lasted for several days and I achieved Nirguna Parabrahman: the state of complete identification with Brahman.

* * *

The word "Paramatman" came to me once. I did not know its meaning. Someone explained it. It was during the time I was in trance for fourteen hours a day. For three days in my trance I repeated the word "Paramatman" and I realized the state.

* * *

One day I felt that the upper part of my brain was opening and expanding. A strange but constant force was filling my brain. If this force stayed there, I felt I could live without food. I believe that if a man remains in a state of trance, he can live without eating.

So I started to practice the state of Samadhi. Sometimes I was in trance for fourteen hours a day. Whomever I thought of I could see clearly, whether they were present or far away. Slowly I learnt how to remain in Samadhi, without going into trance. I achieved a state of dual consciousness, able to move in other worlds while being fully conscious and present in this.

* * *

It was at that time that Mother was travelling frequently to the Supramental Regions, The Kingdom of the Supermind.

* * *

I noticed that the Supramental Beings were different from Gods and from men. They were very tall, and they had a white and rose-tinged complexion. Their bodies were soft, slender, delicate, shining like mirrors and transparent, without bones or nerves. There was no way of telling male from female. As an outer covering, instead of clothing, there was a substance clinging to their bodies as a part of it, and it could be changed at will. Their language was different and not even the Gods could understand it. The articles they used were beautiful, soft and delicate as their bodies. I had thought they did not feed themselves, but I saw a fruit tree and it bore seedless fruits. The Supramental Beings were surprised and saddened by everything human, by the ugliness of man's skeleton, by the range of his vices, by his laziness and unconsciousness and ignorance.

* * *

Once when I returned from the world of Supramental Beings, Durga and Saraswati and Lakshmi asked me eagerly about them. They were very curious. I said, "Why are you asking me? You are omniscient, aren't you?" And then they admitted that they know nothing about the Supramental Beings and their world.

* * *

Once Durga took me to the Supramental World but did not explain anything, didn't enter, and returned home.

Another being took me further and showed me many wonders and miracles. This being did not know my language but we communicated by gestures. Later it placed something snow-white, very soft and crystal-clear and cool in one of my hands and an orange-coloured cloth in the other, and told me that I should keep them with me always.

* * *

On another journey, a group of Supramental Beings met me. Then I was shown around the rooms of a palace by a "professor". One room, which I had already seen, was locked. There were eleven other rooms, each as spacious as a hall. When I was coming out with the "professor" I met the other eleven "professors". They explained all the wonders I had seen to me in my own language. After they explained everything I found that I could understand their language and established a close inner contact with them. I do not think that the human mind is developed enough to enter that world.

* * *

These are some of the essential experiences of Mother in Her fifteenth and sixteenth years. By the end of that time, Mother had merged with several Divine powers; She had experienced Nirguna Parabrahman and Paramatman; She had received gifts from Gods and Rishis of all kinds; She had visited the world of the Supramental Beings and learnt their language.

Experiences of great significance continued through 1978. On February 28 of that year, Mr. Reddy and Mother returned to Pondicherry.

* * *

At that time (1978) I went to the Supramental Plane. It is harder to reach the Supramental Plane than to reach the Overmind.

Great forces and lights from the Supramental Planes descended into me continuously from March 17 to April 15. Before this descent my subtle personality was that of the Goddess Lakshmi, my character that of Durga. After the descent my subtle personality was replaced with white light. The forces themselves were like white clouds, changing into blue and gold. They came day and night. I received from them like a flood, knowledge, light, ananda, and peace.

* * *

One time I saw that Sweet Mother was working in a vast field of earth consciousness and was cleaning it. Sweet Mother had cleansed one fourth of the field, but three fourths remained. Sweet Mother gave me this work, asking me to finish it. That is what I am doing. Into this unfinished part the light must be mixed. By this light the whole earth will be transformed into something as soft as butter. When that is accomplished the Supramental Beings will descend and a new creation will begin.

* * *

On July 9, 1978, light entered into my body through my fingernails, like a procession of ants. It was an indescribable white, blue, red and golden light. A mixture of all these colours. I saw the light pass physically through my fingers. In my eyes I noticed light like the rays of the sun, which created a strange movement in them. When the light entered my body it was shaken as if by an earthquake. My sense organs were cut off and I could neither see nor hear. The light entered every cell. The cells

India 1974

were everywhere jangled by the light, moving and changing in it. I felt the whole process as one of complete cleansing.

It was impossible to control my body. My mind, my heart also became helpless. I felt as if I had no bones or nerves and felt my heart going weaker. I could not pick up any objects, they just fell out of my hands. I could not walk and I felt as if my knees and not my feet were standing on the floor. My body was as weak and supple as a snake and couldn't stand upright.

The experience lasted two hours, from 8 a.m. to 10 a.m. My body changed. It seemed to me that it became very light and no longer was on this earth. Whatever I was doing in the gross physical body I was doing with the help of Sweet Mother. When the experience ended, the whole body remained painful for two days, although my mind and heart went immediately back to normal.

* * *

I understand that the individual physical body and the earth consciousness change every moment in an inexpressible way. This is a crucial time for the earth; many changes will be brought about. It is a supremely auspicious time to receive light. That is why everyone must aspire for it and surrender to the Divine. Now nothing is impossible.

* * *

At 2 a.m. on July 19, 1978, another experience began! I saw a sentence that started with the word "AUM". Each word of the sentence was formed by eight letters in white dazzling light. The sentence appeared in one language after another, from the left, and then moved towards the right and disappeared.

As the sentence moved, I heard music. I felt a great movement in my mind, the cells of the mind rushing around like clouds in the sky. I tried to note down some of the letters in my language, but as I began the script disappeared! I then realized it is impossible for the mind to understand and so my mind went silent. The experience was repeated. I felt my inner being was understanding these scripts in various languages and was enjoying these but my mind could not see them. I felt that a great change was taking place in me and I saw a tremendous power enter into me. I was intoxicated with Ananda.

The experience lasted thirty-six hours. Afterwards I felt pain in my head, a pain moving from one point to another. The pain lasted seven days.

* * *

When Mr. Reddy and the Mother came back to Pondicherry many people were immediately interested in Mother's work and personality. Some were sufficiently interested to ask for Mother's Darshan and ask Her some questions. There were two visits from leading Ashramites in May and June. Each time Mother was asked certain very searching questions. All of those who came were convinced by Her.

The news of Mother's coming was not to be confined merely to the Ashram; in 1978, U.N.I., an Indian Government newspaper, reported it throughout India.

Many letters all over India came to the small house in Pondicherry where Mother, Mr. Reddy and myself were then living, begging Mother's help for every conceivable problem and difficulty, and asking Her many questions about the nature of Her work and identity. It was at this time also that Mother began to collect foreign devotees around Her. Jean-Marc Frechette from Quebec became Her devotee in November; Mother had already been regularly visited by an Englishman, Robert, an Italian, Germans, Americans, French, Russians, and a Japanese. The later part of 1978 was also a time of profound inner change and growth for Mother.

* * *

In August 1978 someone asked me to give a message as Sweet Mother used to at darshan. I did not want to and refused. After nine weeks I felt an inner force compel me to write the following message:

Love Paramatman.
Ask the Lord for His shakti.
Pray to God to overcome your difficulties.
Aspire to be His children.

If you ask wholeheartedly He will answer your prayer. Your ego is useless before the Supreme though it may be of some use to human beings for some time but not always. You are small children before Him. The Lord is above all Gods, all Goddesses, all Rishis and Avadhutas. He is supreme. Therefore pray to the Lord only. If you do not have the power or the Shakti to pray directly to the Supreme, ask those who have it. If you are conscious that a person has the Paramatman Shakti, then ask that person.

If your mind hesitates to ask the person who possesses that Shakti, put your doubts aside, come forward and ask.

Hurry, Hurry. Awaken! Be conscious;
Come forward and help the world!
The earth is waiting for the Light.

* * *

Mother says:

Our body is an instrument and servant to our consciousness. Our consciousness is quite free from the body and will function according to its condition. It will work in and beyond time, in and beyond space, in darkness as in light, in form as in formlessness. The soul is free from limits. Our field of consciousness is full of action, without words. It bears an ocean of knowledge. It is without rest.

Our body moves here as a machine, our consciousness moves everywhere, without hindrance. Whatever is accomplished with the body without a higher consciousness is purely nominal and has no value. But with the aid of the higher consciousness its work is important to the Divine Play. Nothing can affect our consciousness, which moves and acts without the body. There will therefore be no change in its action after death, for if the body vanishes, our consciousness does not disappear. Within or without the body, we are always in consciousness.

This experience occurred at 7:40 p.m. on December 7, 1978:

I knew the path to the Paramatman but I wanted to follow Him in the new way. I saw Sri Aurobindo in infinitely dazzling Lights and I went up to him. After a moment of silence he spoke, "Why have you come here?" "I came for a purpose," I replied. And I was about to return when I realized suddenly that I had come here very often without seeing Paramatman. I told Sri Aurobindo, "I want to see Paramatman." He answered, "After seeing Him what will you do? Will you stay with Him or return?" "I will do whatever I feel I should," I said. But Sri Aurobindo said, "You never know what you might feel." I said, "I will obey Paramatman in everything." Sri Aurobindo disappeared. I remained with Paramatman for some time. I thought, "Even though I remain for a long time I will have to go back, so what is the use of staying here!" So I left.

I saw Sri Aurobindo sitting on the ground. His hands were stretched out. He was resting his right hand on a rough surface of rocks and thorns, his left hand on a smooth surface. I said that the right hand was Sri Aurobindo's but the left one was Sweet Mother's. "Oh," said Sri Aurobindo, "then you recognized them. This rough surface also must be transformed so it becomes smooth. This is the work we have to do."

* * *

I hadn't felt well since October 19, 1978, and it was now October 24. First I felt that Adishakti, the Supreme Mother, had descended in the world. Then I heard that She would descend. Finally, Adishakti appeared in front of me. She came close to me and called me "Mother" and then "Child". I too went up to Her and called Her "Mother". She looked at me with absolute concentration for an hour. She held my hands. I bowed down at Her lotus feet; I saw Her form disappear and then, whenever I looked, I could see golden light. I was conscious of this in my inner being, not my outer mind.

The experience which lasted six days seemed only to last one day. After Adishakti had disappeared I saw the golden light with my physical as well as my inner sight. The only difference was in the intensity of the light. I was in great joy.

When Adishakti identified with me I saw Mother Durga and Sri Aurobindo and many other Gods and Goddesses.

* * *

This experience happened at Kali Puja, on October 31, 1978:

I was near Sweet Mother when she told me: "On the Holy Days, ask the Gods and Goddesses to bestow more abundantly than usual upon the earth their power and light, not limiting themselves to the Supramental powers. They do not yield to the requests of ordinary human beings, but they heed the prayers of Divine personalities. So ask all of them on their Holy Days." I consented.

Sri Aurobindo asked me: "Meera, are you asking the Gods for more power for the earth?" I replied: "I am asking for Light, nothing else." He went on: "Ask all the Gods for it. There is Light enough to accomplish the earthly transformation, but with the grace of the Gods the work could be hastened."

I was leaving and saw someone who looked like Mahakali; she was very beautiful. When I saw her face, I recognized Mahakali's bliss, her great power and passion. I approached her and expressed my wish. Mahakali exclaimed: "I know who has sent you here!" I asked for more power, more light, more peace to give to the world. "Do you need these for yourself or for the world?" I answered: "I myself have enough of them since I am getting what I need. I want more for the earth." Mahakali smiled, left without any answer. She had crossed the earthly plane in a sort of enchantment, very swiftly, as if carelessly. I was puzzled and felt uneasy before her strange behavior, not knowing if she wanted to protect or destroy the world. But I said: "Mother, I must tell you something." "What is it?" she asked. "I want more of your power."

I moved on a bit further when I noticed something that looked like a hard white stone – although I did not know the name the Gods gave it. I clasped the stone in my hands. A white light came from it and went up into the sky. I thought: "When there is already plenty of light above, why should I allow this light to go up also?" I covered the stone with my hands blocking the light. Then all the light descended on the earth which blossomed like a white lotus. I moved on as the blossom spread far and wide. I thought, "I have begun the work and it will achieve its results. It is not necessary that I remain here. If the process ceases then I will come back to start it again."

Further on I met Ishwara. The trisul (trident) was between my neck and navel. I also saw a small baby, who was suffering and smiling at the same time. Its face expressed sorrow, pain, delight and power. When I touched the baby I saw a light so bright that I closed my eyes. And suddenly I was brought to the Supramental World.

Leaving the Supramental World I crossed three worlds beyond the Supramental Plane (beyond these three worlds: Sat, Chit, Ananda, is the Paramatman). I strongly felt that something could be brought down from this region, but saw nothing concrete there. "All right," I thought, "Let it be." I descended from the three planes.

Then my body changed; I felt I had no soul, no mind, and had become so light that I was flying. I finally reached Sweet Mother and Sri Aurobindo with a gathering of Supramental Beings. The Supramental Beings rose and disappeared. I was left alone, floating as in the wind, thinking: "What is being kept hidden here? They have all brought something and hidden it here. No one gives it to the world. Why?" Meanwhile Sweet Mother appeared: "Meera, what are you searching for?" "The world is in need of more light," I answered. Sweet Mother objected and said that the world craved for riches, not light. I pleaded: "I am not concerned with wealth. But the world needs more light."

Sri Aurobindo's form – not his body – was seen descending. I was pulling on this form to make it descend on earth, but it did not penetrate the earth. The form turned and rose up again. "Why is the form not penetrating the earth?" I thought. "Oh! How we have sinned." I was deeply sad. "But," I thought, "Sri Aurobindo and Sweet Mother have come to this earth to transform it and will surely accomplish their work. Sweet Mother has entrusted me to ask the Gods for more power and light on their Holy Days. I shall carry on." Upon approaching Mahakali I felt: "Why should I interfere with the Gods' work? The earth is already becoming more supple, more plastic." "What do you want, Meera?" asked Mahakali. "Power, energy, light and the power to love everything," I answered. "I can bestow on you the power to love all," Mahakali replied, "but not the other powers." I insisted: "Give me whatever you have, light, energy, power. If you give me only love, then I will think you have no powers." And Mahakali answered: "All right! I will see what is possible." We gazed at each other for a while.

Mahakali held out a finger and I clasped it. Sound was emanating from her finger, like "AUM", which produced a light from which a force or power and bliss emanated. I returned to Sweet Mother to explain what had been experienced. She was happy, and I came down to earth.

I saw there a person with a huge body. I hesitated: "How could I carry such a body to the higher planes, I am so small," I thought. I found it not delicate to touch this person and just gazed at her. The person became a small child. The inner force compelled me to touch it and take it in my arms. Its face changed into a yellow and golden colour. I moved on with the child, meeting Sri Aurobindo, Krishna, Rama, Durga, Jesus, Mary, Ramakrishna Paramahamsa, Vivekananda, and others. They were greeting my ascent and pushing me on. I was soaring up as if I was caught in a whirlwind, higher and higher still. Then slowly I descended and met Sweet Mother. I gave the body to Sweet Mother and spoke to Sri Aurobindo who was sitting nearby, explaining that I found it unpleasant to touch such full grown bodies since I was so small. "How can I love these huge bodies?" I asked. "We don't have to bother about their bodies," Sri Aurobindo answered, "nor their intellects. We are concerned with their souls and powers only." Sri Aurobindo insisted that I love the older people and not the children, since the children have already a psychic opening. I agreed.

Continuing my descent, I met a poet sitting under a tree. This poet was all-knowing, he possessed the wisdom of the physical, vital, mental, overmental, and supramental worlds, and was aware of the good and evil forces. He could write on all subjects. And he was writing now under the tree. I was compelled by an inner force to approach him, but hesitated before his huge body. How could I tell him of my intention to bring him to the higher worlds? When I stood in front of him he reverently offered his Pranams. "Mother, would You like to take all of us to the higher worlds?" he asked. I nodded. He agreed to accompany me but I interrupted: "I will take all of you at once to the higher worlds, but not one at a time." He asked: "And after taking us there, who will take care of us? Is Your power sufficient to purify us?" I replied: "I have the power but I must follow my inner will. If it wishes to uplift the whole of humanity, with my power I can do it."

I went on descending, accompanied by Sweet Mother and Sri Aurobindo. I thought: "If I stay any longer, the human world will not receive sufficient light for its change. I have seen the three planes beyond the Supramental and did not find what I needed. There is something still invisible beyond these planes which I must get." Yet I wondered why I must love all mankind and uplift it. I felt I had accepted this ordeal and resolved to reach for the invisible beyond. On a higher plane Sri Aurobindo asked me: "Meera, have you done your duty?" I replied: "I do not feel like

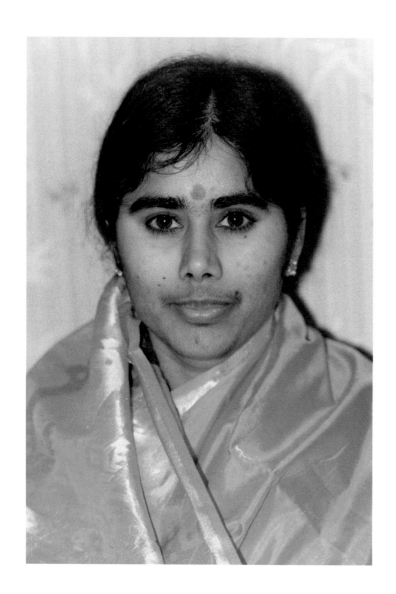

Thalheim, Germany 1994

finishing the work. I am interested in something else which I could fulfill. Above the Supramental Plane there are three worlds. Beyond them, on a fourth plane, there is something that ought to be brought down. Everything there is invisible. I see nothing. I don't know how to bring this thing down. Maybe you would know." Sri Aurobindo said he was ready to help and offered to accompany me. "I leave it to your will and pleasure," I said. Sri Aurobindo then added that Sweet Mother might be going there. I smiled at him. He continued: "Why don't you go with some Supramental Beings instead of us?" I found no objection at all to this, but could not find the way to ask the Supramental Beings gathered with Sri Aurobindo and Sweet Mother. The Beings themselves called upon a charming lady which Sri Aurobindo asked to accompany me. We left together.

The climbing was difficult. On the fourth plane, on my first trip, I had found the place full of light. But now, it was deadly dark and the object that I was searching for had disappeared. I felt dreadful and very frightened. I thought: "What am I to do with this darkness, even if I pass through it?" I saw a light and decided that I would bring either the light or the darkness with me. By then the Supramental lady had left and I was alone. I saw witches, asuras, devils, evil spirits, quarrelling and acting in a chaotic fashion. They wanted to provoke me to some reaction so that they could retaliate against me. I stood aloof and quiet. All disappeared.

Then I wandered with hands clasped behind my back, majestically, powerfully, and cheerfully. I knew intuitively that victory was mine and mine alone. I intensified my will with fervent aspiration, concentrating powerfully to bring back this power to earth so as to transform it. While descending I heard ten times: "You will get it!" Later I heard the same voice twice again.

I reached Sweet Mother and Sri Aurobindo who were sitting on the ground. I stood beside them. "What, Meera!" they said, smiling faintly. I talked with them about their resolution to uplift humanity, of the time it would take, of the amount of power which had to be poured into human beings for their transformation, and into the evil forces of the higher worlds, of the necessity to implore the Goddesses to be generous in their help. Sri Aurobindo remarked that only if these preliminary conditions were fulfilled could they be benevolent towards humanity. Sweet Mother interrupted by asking if humanity could be happy and peaceful, if all men were full of devotion. And I said that too much leniency had been shown which permitted humanity to be prodigal: "If we had condemned them then and there, they could not have cultivated such arrogance, but instead might have cultivated devotion and reverence." Sri Aurobindo left, upwards, pointing his finger. I descended to earth.

* * *

This long and central experience was followed just a month later by a special descent of the Supramental Light – November 21, 1978. Mother announced on that date that there would be a special descent of Supramental Light. Between 5:30 and 6:00 p.m. the Light descended with immense force for a minute. It then took two hours to be established in the earth's atmosphere. Usually, Mother says, the Light is sent by Sri Aurobindo to Sweet Mother who in turn sends it to the earth. On that day, for the first time to Mother Meera's knowledge, the Supramental Beings themselves sent the Supramental Light to the Overmind beings (Durga, Saraswati, Krishna), and Vivekananda, Jesus, Ramakrishna Paramahamsa who in turn sent it to the earth, and to all who are receptive on the earth. They also, Mother said, forcefully infused the light into those who were not receptive.

When asked about how the light enters the body, Mother said:

It enters from above the head, through the fingernails or through the soles of the feet. Wherever it enters, it produces a burning sensation and that part of the body feels numbness. If the body is not strong physically, severe pain is felt for ten to fifteen minutes, as severe as a scorpion sting. Those who are unwilling or unreceptive feel the pain especially. When the body is fully charged with light, even though the pain is severe it should not try to reject the light. On the contrary, aspiration for it must grow, despite its effects. The pain may last for ten or fifteen minutes but will vanish completely after two hours. Afterwards a supreme Joy and Peace will be felt and all obstacles to the furthest spiritual progress will be removed. You will know that you have received the light because you will experience love to all humanity and an infinite concern for all life. You will want to work to save the world and at the same time feel a complete and peaceful detachment from the world.

* * *

It was in January 1979 that Mother called down onto the earth the Paramatman Light and made the transformation of the world certain. Mother had seen that another light was essential if the world was to be changed: now She brought it down onto the earth.

After the descent of the Supramental Light in November, Mother said:

To transform the world I am going to bring down the Light from Paramatman. And this will make transformation go much faster. Sweet Mother and Sri Aurobindo are inspiring me in this work and anticipating the descent of this highest Light.

Paramatman is beyond the three worlds that lie above the Supramental World. It is there that I have seen the special Light and willed to bring it down to earth.

She added in late November:

If in addition to the Supramental Beings, the Paramatman also sends His Light, it will be excellent for the work. I have been told to ask for His Light. Be conscious always. Love the Paramatman. Be like children in His presence. Pray to Him to remove all your difficulties.

At the end of December Mother told Her disciples the following:

For ninety days I have seen a Divine Mother. I felt that She was Adishakti, the Supreme Mother, because She was everything in Her light – peace, force and power. This Mother has descended and appeared to me and I bowed at Her feet. When I bowed down I felt I was freeing myself completely and going to higher worlds. I then thought this could happen in the physical world so all humanity can be uplifted and saved by it. May my desire be accomplished quickly...

When I am with this Divine Mother I am in the form of Mahalakshmi. No one can match my beauty and I have the power to love everything and to uplift everything. When I compare myself with Her I find myself more beautiful and more powerful. She does not look beautiful but has everything in Her. What is manifest in me is hidden in Her. When I think of the mystery of this I am filled with joy...

On December 31 I fell at the feet of Mother Adishakti and pressed Her lotus feet with devotion. Slowly Adishakti moved away and gradually descended. After Her departure I became more powerful, more full of love. The last trace of fear in me disappeared.

But I was not satisfied. I was still looking for something, I did not know what...

Mother then told us:

On December 30 and 31, 1978, I, Sweet Mother and Sri Aurobindo, Durga, Saraswati, Ramakrishna Paramahamsa, Vivekananda, Jesus, Mary, and others met to control the evil forces that were threatening the world. These forces yielded slightly but not completely. After we had met they became very violent and renewed their attack. I approached them. I learned that they wanted to attack me physically. I was indifferent to that at first, but went to Paramatman. I prayed to Paramatman. "You are in everything, Lord. You should control the evil forces. You alone must send Your Light onto earth. You are in everything, so Your Light should be in everything." Then I heard a voice, "You should not ask alone." So I went to Sweet Mother and Sri Aurobindo and told them. They agreed that they too would pray to Paramatman. And Durga, Lakshmi, Saraswati, Ganapati, Ishwara, Krishna, Rama, Vivekananda also agreed, with other Gods and Goddesses and Avatars. Prayers started on January 1, 1979. We all implored Paramatman with folded hands and then with outstretched hands. But no Light appeared. It stayed dark. We went on praying. Then a spark of Light appeared and we were assured of His presence. We prayed very reverently. He blessed our prayer and said that the Light could descend.

Then I and all the others sent the Light to the dark worlds where the evil forces are powerful and the Light also descended on the whole earth and into all hearts ready to receive it.

Nevertheless we continued praying: "Paramatman, You are everywhere. Everything is Yours. Remove our difficulties. We have come here easily, safely and even though we have suffered we have received what we asked for. But some have suffered more and still remain unblessed. Make them happy also. Remove all their difficulties. Give them peace." Paramatman heard and accepted the prayer.

* * *

The result of these events and experiences was that on January 2, 1979, at 3:00 p.m. the Light, colourless but dazzling, began to descend little by little from Paramatman. By 5:00 p.m. it had increased its descent. Wherever the asuric forces were most powerful on earth, the Light descended most rapidly to conquer them. Mother said:

The Light descends but it is already everywhere! In every cell! All must be open to it. There is resistance in the world to the Supramental Light which causes pain in the body; but the Paramatman Light does not burn the body. It fills with ecstasy!

Mother added:

When the Paramatman Light descends, with delight and peace, it brings a deeper silence. And it descends without intermediaries.

Mother then gave us this message:

I thought that the asuric forces would be completely extinguished. But still some evil forces remain. We must aspire with all our wills and hearts to Paramatman so that these too may be extinguished. Remember that we all have the Paramatman Shakti within us. We have to try and reveal that Light which is hidden in us as a bud. It must blossom like a flower. In all things everywhere, in all beings the Light is hidden, and it must be revealed. If we try with all our hearts we will be successful. Then we will be able to go to the higher worlds and have the Darshan of the Gods. We will live perpetually in the Paramatman Light and be Paramatman. I want the Paramatman Light to blossom everywhere.

* * *

The whole purpose of Mother Meera's work is in this calling down of the Light, it is for this that She came; it is to open our hearts to this Light that Her mission on earth was begun. Our entire purpose, as Her devotees, and as lovers of the world, is to open with all our being to this Light. If we open to it, She has promised, it will work with amazing swiftness and force within us; its miracle of transformation will be achieved within us. That is Her promise and Her will.

* * *

The Paramatman Light descended on January 2, 1979; in September 1979 Mother went for Her first visit abroad to Canada. The intervening months were spent in Pondicherry. This experience took place on January 9, 1979:

Daily people meditate in the presence of Mother Meera from 4:30 p.m. to 6:30 p.m. At 5:25 p.m. today, Mother Meera, feeling weak, asked to be excused for a moment of rest. Someone asked Her: "Since you never leave us in the middle of meditation, may we please know why you are asking for a rest today?"

Mother explained to us the following process happened only at this time and would never be repeated in the future:

Since in my inner activities I look after many planes at a time, there are many reasons; I will explain one of them.

In the higher planes is a place that collects all the qualities and aspects of being which are rejected by us. Generally these can be refined there, but, if not, they are sent to the necessary planes for their refinement. I took you all to this plane.

There, two beings live, who are managing all these things, and more especially the Divine powers like light, peace, bliss and knowledge. All these qualities are mixed together and the mixture shines with a powerful and dazzling Light. The mixtures are capsuled into small units, about three inches long. Even a single ray from one of them has a great force.

One of the Beings opened the skull of each of you, and the other fixed this dazzling Divine Process inside the head. It must reach the feet; as it moves downwards it dislocates the cells and creates a great vibration in the body, giving it a burning sensation, and by the help of our Sadhana, it starts to move upwards. Then it will burn up the human nature and, one by one, all its undivine qualities. The power of the Divine, given to us in it, will then develop with the progress of our Sadhana. These powers are set as a seed in an undeveloped condition in us, and will grow with our Sadhana.

The all-powerful Divine Light will be given only once to a human being, and it will be his foundation for the Divine life. It will continue its work for many lives, if it is necessary, until we become Divine. It is not given to all, but only to those who are recommended by Divine Personalities or Avatars.

Generally we aspire for one or a few divine qualities such as Light, Peace or Bliss. And usually we receive them one by one. But with the special method of the Divine Light, we get all the divine qualities in the form of seeds. By our sincere Sadhana, these seeds will be transformed into trees.

We have said that when the Divine Light is fixed in the head and establishes itself in the body, the body suffers some uneasiness, inconvenience, pain – as a burning sensation. The pain should not trouble us; we should not reject the Divine Light under any circumstances. If, having received the Light, we are not sincere and do nothing to develop the divine seeds consciously, they will remain hidden within us.

On April 12, 1979, Mother told us of the descent of the Paramatman Light in a different, solid form:

Previously the Paramatman Light and the Supramental Light were descending everywhere onto the earth like sunlight or snow. Because of that descent, the whole earth has been flowering. From today the Light is concentrated in solid form. In large blocks and small ones these blazing forms of concentrated light are dropped onto the earth according to need and aspiration. They are piercing the surface of the earth and penetrating deeper and deeper into the earth. The earth, as a result, is beginning to open from within and to blossom even more completely. In January the Light was brought down – now in this different form. The Light is effecting the transformation even more rapidly.

* * *

On June 23, 1979, Mother told us:

Beside a pond I saw a higher being. The water in the pond glittered with yellow light. Then other colours appeared: orange, blue, red and white. The higher being disappeared leaving a path upon the water that led very high and far towards many planes. There were houses of golden colour, from one of which came a woman in a red sari. She seemed about forty, her body was flooded with orange light, and she was radiant. I tried to meet her, but couldn't.

Then I heard a voice saying I should go in a certain direction. I went but no one else was there, I had no sense of which plane it was, because all the worlds were there. It was as if all the people there were transformed and so all the planes could be seen there: Overmind, Supermind, and other worlds.

I felt like going somewhere, but I did not know where exactly. Then suddenly I heard a sound behind me and observed from where it was coming, a place where I had been before and which was very neat and clean. Feeling an intense desire to see

Paramatman, I fell silent, and then a Mother came and stood before me. I did not know how to surrender to her. Usually, whenever I have met such beings, I have surrendered to them spontaneously my body, mind and soul. But today I did not feel at all like surrendering to that Mother, although she seemed great and powerful, with abundant energy, and had access to all the planes of being.

When she was in front of me, at first she had two hands, but later she had many hands and heads. Beneath her feet was a huge serpent, supporting her as the earth supports our feet. Water was flowing from her hands and her body as she jumped and played upon the serpent. Then poison began oozing from the serpent's mouth.

I felt that this Mother, as the water flowed from her body, was cleansing human beings of their impurities, and I asked her how to make myself worthy of helping her. "Be awake and aware always of the Divine, who is very merciful to you. Are you ready to obey me?" I said yes, joyfully, and she told me to take all the poison coming from the serpent and offer it to Paramatman. But I thought, "If the Supreme is in all things, surely He is in this poison also." I collected the poison and poured it into a vessel. When I touched it, I saw the Paramatman Light shining from it. This made me very happy. Then the poison became very thick, and filled the vessel.

After this I could tell that I was moving on the Overmind Plane. On the way I saw some swans, who followed me and to some extent showed me the direction to go. As I proceeded I saw a huge, brightly-lit building. Some higher beings were coming out through its entrance. They were smiling. They were not Gods, and I hesitated to offer the poison to them. Suddenly some of them moved aside, making room for me to enter the building. Inside I saw Paramatman, who was full of light, and offered Him the poison. It was immediately changed into some sacred substance, which will be kept there and given to human beings when they are divine.

I returned to the Mother I had seen before and told her all that had happened. "Whatever we need, it is Paramatman who can give it to us, Mother," she told me tenderly. "He is the supreme giver-of-gifts, there is no one like Him."

* * *

And then Mother told us on June 26, 1979:

Today Paramatman called me and I went to Him. Everything around Him was so beautiful that I wanted to stay with Him and not return. So I asked Paramatman: "The last time I came here I wanted to stay with You forever, now I want to stay with You even more intensely... What is Your will?"

He replied: "There are other souls to come and stay with me." So I asked Him what I should do. "Consecrate to Me your soul, which has resolved to be forever with Me." I said that since I had surrendered my soul to Him I needed another to guard and care for my body. Then He told me: "When you feel like consecrating your soul, tell Me, and I will endow you with a powerful soul not only to look after your body but also to fulfill the purpose of your Avatarhood."

After hearing these words from the Supreme I wanted to return to earth. "You have changed my mind in spite of my determination to remain permanently with You. It is a good thing for You to alter my will in this way. I also change human beings who have bad wills and bad characters." Paramatman replied: "You have great power and skill. For that reason I decided that you should be on earth to fulfill your mission as an Avatar. This is essential for the earth."

Then I asked: "The Avadhutas or realized persons who renounce all the worlds and planes and all the powers come to You and stay. Do You send them back to earth at any time or in any age? And if they return to earth, do they have devotees?" Paramatman then explained to me: "Ordinarily they do not like to return to earth. I send them when they are needed. They do not

Thalheim, Germany 1984

need disciples; people may not even know who they are or where they live."

"Why do they live on earth without being known?" I asked. "When they are known does this cause them pain? Is their work disturbed by a large number of devotees? Are devotees an obstacle in the working out of their mission?" He replied: "Even though they may be known, they are not understood correctly or recognized as Avadhutas. And when people understand them a little only, this can cause them more trouble. The more disciples they have, the more the Avadhutas concentrate on them rather than on their mission of uplifting the world. They uplift only their devotees. So naturally they prefer not to have devotees."

Then I asked Paramatman: "As spirituality grows, our mind and vital parts become weak. Why is this?" He replied: "The physical, vital and mental abilities are changed into a greater power. Therefore these normal parts of the human being become weak, as they surrender their strength to that spiritual power. When a man is highly developed spiritually, and ordinary devotees who are dominated by the mind and vital forces come to him, he is often unwilling to see or talk with them because moving among such people seems so strange."

* * *

On August 22, 1979, Mother told us:

Since August 12 I have been feeling my body becoming much lighter, as if floating in the air. In spite of my pressing it downwards it insists on flying. There have also been some peculiar movements inside my body, making me very uncomfortable, a kind of pain moving from one part to another, like the fish and snakes that disappear in one place in a pond or river only to reappear at another place.

On the night of August 22, when I lay down at 10:30, severe pains surged up in my right chest. Later the same pains were felt in my left thigh. For a while I could not move my body, but later I was able to turn on my side. I felt someone was calling, trying to awaken me, but no one was there.

The electric light was on in my room, but in spite of that I saw a bright, luminous light focusing on me from a distance. I gazed at it with increasing concentration. Both sides of the light were adorned with beautiful flowers like Shivalingams, and the light was coming towards me between those two flowers. As I gazed at the light I felt drunk with happiness, coolness and peace.

Then I sensed that the light was going to enter into me. There was some resistance in my right foot, but through the left foot it entered me easily. There was a kind of mild irritation in the whole body, but afterwards I felt again the intoxicating peace and happiness.

The body became very agile. Even while walking I felt that my feet were not touching the floor. All the pains that had bothered me for so long were greatly diminished and I felt energetic and full of delight.

Paramatman told me the following: "Up until now you have been able to see Me and talk with Me, but My Light had not entered your body. Now I am filling your body with My Light, and I shall go on filling it with Light."

After this experience I see the Paramatman Light unceasingly.

* * *

Then Mother Meera told the following experience on February 2, 1979. For four days, Mother Meera had felt the inspiration to narrate the birth of the four aspects of Durga:

In the very beginning, Durga went to Paramatman and asked Him to give her more forms of existence. She asked for the first form and Paramatman sanctioned her request. This form was named Mahalakshmi and Paramatman described its attributes. Thus was Mahalakshmi born.

Then Durga asked for the forms of Mahasaraswati and Maheshvari. Paramatman approved once more and specified their qualities. Durga accepted them.

Afterwards she asked for a special form, and Paramatman, giving no description this time, merely said, "Do as you wish." And a unique, powerful, victorious and unchallengeable form was born.

Durga came to Paramatman vested in this last form. She was decorated with ornaments, a most beautiful attire and a gorgeous sari. But taking leave of Paramatman, she appeared naked and dancing. She was charming and beautiful, free to do as she wished. This form was Mahakali who has such tremendous powers. If she chooses she can lift the sincere devotees to the highest planes effortlessly, or can give the power of victory in all battles. But if the devotees lack in sincerity, while other Gods may excuse them, Mahakali does not tolerate it. She does not pardon insincerity and punishes without mercy, to the point of heaving the insincere into an abyss.

* * *

On August 30, 1979, Mother told us:

In the morning I had this fear. In my frequent journeys to the higher worlds, who will safeguard me if I fall, since I am not making any effort for my security?

That evening, during meditation, I felt a kind of falling movement in my body, as if slipping from a great height. Instantaneously, as if responding to an impending fall, the Paramatman Light, Supramental Light and Overmental Lights poured down upon me in a powerful flood, causing a kind of movement in my body. This gave me an intense feeling of security, like a promise from the Supreme that all the lights of the higher worlds would encompass me, to help me and guard me.

* * *

By the end of 1979 Mother's identification with the Supreme Mother was complete; She had succeeded in bringing down on earth the light of the Supreme Lord that makes transformation certain; She had been assured of the Paramatman's help and protection and power in everything She undertook.

* * *

On July 23, 1980, the Mother told the following experience:

The Light is bursting out from me as a great tremendous sound like thunder and dazzling like bright sunlight... I am sending Light like this everywhere three times a day. The Light is covering the whole earth. When the Light leaves my body, it leaves it with such an enormous sound that I cannot hear for two hours afterwards. This process is going on.

In August 1980, the Mother told us:

Sometimes I feel my feet are burning as though I am walking on fire, even when I am walking on water on the floor, wherever I am walking. Now I am "the Mother of Fire". This is because of the Light I am giving to the earth. It is working dynamically. The earth is responding to it more deeply than human beings.

THE DESCENT OF LIGHT (IN ITS ASPECT OF LOVE) IN APRIL AND MAY 1983

During the preceding months of April and May, a great descent of Light took place. The goal of the descent was to manifest the divine love. For Mother Meera's body, this descent was a period of terrible difficulty. We are very grateful to Mother Meera for assuming for us all this work of manifestation.

Great and happy news concerning the descent of light which lasted two months; now the descent is finished. This Light came specially to manifest Love. During the descent Mother had the impression that Her body was like an empty bottle and that the Light was like a liquid. When a bottle is agitated the liquid rises, descends, moves in all sides. It is thus, when the Mother's body was agitated, the Light penetrated in the body and turned and moved in all directions. The whole body was as if annihilated. At that moment the Mother did not feel any pain and

She was "somewhere", we do not know where. If we called Her, She did not answer, for She was very far away. All the function of Her senses were stopped. The entire body was shaken, legs and arms moving in all directions.

At the beginning the descent of Light used to start at midnight and lasted until six in the morning. Then Mother rested afterwards for one hour or two. During the whole day, She was back to normal. But, after a few days the descent of Light became as strong during the day as during the night. From that moment the Mother knew neither sleep nor rest and She did not take any food. She constantly felt in the body a pain intolerable for human beings. When the pain was too great, the Mother became unconscious.

We were scared and wanted to call a doctor. When we asked the Mother if we could call a doctor She answered "NO", and became again unconscious. Later Mother explained to us that during this state Her senses did not function. When we asked Her what was Her condition She did not reply because our questions did not reach Her; if we asked could we bring Her a doctor, the word "doctor" sounded in Her ears like a church bell, for it was not correct to call a doctor. So She came back to our level of consciousness to say "NO" and again She returned to a superior plane. That was because we were not supposed to make the mistake of calling the doctor who, in any case, would not have been useful. He would not have found any reasons for which Mother's body reacted in such a terrible way.

During the last of the descent this Light was so concrete and so solid that we too felt very strongly the atmosphere of Love in the entire house which was filled with Joy.

In this atmosphere, only one hour of sleep is sufficient even for human beings.

There is a big change in Mother's body. It gives the impression of having become as soft as velvet and it is shining.

Now the Mother is very well. She says that a descent of Light of a similar nature will reoccur in two or three years.

The Mother left India for the first time in September 1979 for Canada with Mr. Reddy and myself. We stayed there for four months. Every evening there was Darshan of the Mother. Sometimes personal interviews with the Mother were granted. Every Saturday, in a large auditorium, there was Darshan for sometimes as many as three hundred people. Many people had wonderful experiences. Some saw the Mother as the Virgin Mary, others saw Her as Jesus, or Buddha or Krishna, or as Sri Aurobindo, Sweet Mother, Kali, or Durga. Nearly everyone felt calm and peace. Some experienced Light in different colours – white, blue, gold, orange, violet – according to their development and need. We were happy during our stay in Canada.

On the way back to India, Mother, at the request of certain devotees, visited Switzerland. Then we returned to India. We heard while in India that the Mother Meera Society had been founded in Canada. In February 1981, the Society invited Mother, Mr. Reddy, and me to Canada. We went and the darshans and interviews continued as before. The response to Mother was very great.

Later in the year some German devotees invited Mother and us to Germany. We arrived in August and Mother gave Darshan to a small but very loving group of devotees, many of whom had wonderful experiences of Her love and light. Then in September we returned to Canada. Mr. Reddy's health at this time was beginning to decline. We decided to return to India in October.

German devotees of Mother asked Her to stop again in Germany on Her way back to India. She agreed and we came to Germany at the end of October, and stayed in Kleinmaischeid. Mr. Reddy's health got worse. He went into the hospital. He was diagnosed as having malfunctioning kidneys and dialysis was advised. Due to this turn in Mr. Reddy's health it was impossible to go back to India, so the Mother stayed on in Germany. Mr. Reddy had to go for dialysis three times a week.

In 1982 Mother married a German and he is now staying with the Mother. In 1983 Mother, at Mr. Reddy's request, bought a house. She selected a house in Thalheim, fifteen kilometers from Limburg. Mr. Reddy told Mother he wanted a house in a valley. Thalheim is in a valley. When people told him that "Thal" means "valley" and "heim" "house" he was happy. In Kleinmaischeid Mother used to give Darshan every day. Now She gives it four days a week.

In April 1988 Mother visited India. Many devotees welcomed Mother in Her homeland. In 1989, Hobart and William Smith Colleges in Geneva, New York invited Mother to America. This is the first time Mother visited America. She also visited Ithaca and New York City. In 1990, Mother again visited America and Canada. The Canadian devotees are always eager for Her Darshan because of Her infrequent visits. In November Mother also visited India.

India 1976

HUMAN GLIMPSES OF THE MOTHER

I would like to speak of Mother in Her human personality as I have come to know and love it. The play of the Divine in human form is a delightful mystery. Everything that Mother does on the human plane reveals subtly and warmly another aspect of Her Self and Work.

Sometimes in our conversations Mother has told me a few things about Her childhood.

When Mother was ten, a man, a Koyaraju, a head of a tribe and someone who knew the future, came where Mother was. He told Her that She would live far from Her parents; that She would be worshipped and famous when young; that She was a Goddess with the gift of turning all things She touched to gold.

I have no doubt that Mother is an incarnation of Adiparashakti Herself. Even in Her earliest childhood She saw the Divine Light as we see lightning in the clouds. Whenever She suffered any difficulty or illness, the Divine Light would bless and heal Her.

Mother's visions and mystical powers came to Her spontaneously. This was so even in Her childhood when drops of nectar (Amrita binduvulu) oozed from the brahma randra (the point – or chakra – at the top of the head through which we can achieve realization). Mother knew even then that without taking any food She could, from these nectar drops, be provided with all the energy She needed.

The Mother has never meditated – whom would She meditate on since She is everything? Her Divine Powers came to Her naturally. She cannot be said to be in any of the states of waking, dreaming, sleeping or samadhi at any time. She is above all these four states.

From Her earliest childhood Mother has had a great love for all aspects of the natural world. Nature is the manifestation of the Divine Mother, Her Gift, Her Body.

As a little girl Mother used to go into the forest to be alone. There She would often sit in the hollows of trees. Most children would have been afraid of such places full as they might be of snakes or scorpions. Mother never had any fear. The solitude was delightful to Her.

Mother loves all flowers and animals equally. Her love is tender, practical, and unbounded. I would like to share with you some incidents of this love.

Once we were in India, in Kakinada. It was raining heavily outside. The roads were full of water. Mother, Mr. Reddy and I were in the house talking. Suddenly Mother got up and went into the rain. We were very surprised until we saw that there was a kitten on the doorstep shivering with cold and in a pitiable state. Mother took it tenderly into Her hands, where it died. I feel She had heard its inner call to die in the hands of the Divine and answered it.

In Kakinada, also, the owner of the house had two dogs, a big Alsatian and a small dog that were very affectionate. Whenever the owner was angry with them they would run to Mother for refuge.

Animals can see the Divine clearly. Generally, they are afraid of human beings, of their inner violence and hostility, but in the case of Saints, like Saint Francis or Ramakrishna, or of Incarnations like Mother Herself, they have no fear.

Once in Germany in winter, a baby swallow came into the house. It was shivering and could not fly. Mr. Reddy was ill at the time, lying upstairs. Mother gave him his medicine, came downstairs, picked up the swallow gently then took it to show Mr. Reddy and gave it some warm milk. After a few minutes, it recovered. How delicately She fed it and wiped the water from its wings! Her compassion for helpless things is infinite.

Animals not only recognize the Divine, they also obey it. Once in Thalheim Mother and I were walking. A black cat was following us. Mother turned and said, "Go home." Immediately the cat turned and went home.

One evening in Kakinada Mother was pulling grass out in the garden. A dog came and watched Her. Mother told the dog to come and help Her pull out the grass. It obeyed and everyone around was amazed.

Two of the happiest memories I have of Mother's love of animals have to do with monkeys. As lovers of the Ramayana know, monkeys are particularly sensitive to the Divine.

In 1980 Mother, Mr. Reddy and I were in Nizamabad. We went to the public park. The monkeys there are usually timid but they gathered around Mother to eat peanuts from Her hand.

In January 1981, we were in Madanapalle. There are many monkeys there and they are not friendly. Yet in the early morning they would come silently to see Mother. They made signs that they wanted prasad (the food given by the Divine). Mother would come out of Her room onto the balcony where they waited for Her Darshan and food. She would give them bananas, sweets, groundnuts and other fruit which they would receive, giggling happily. They came regularly and each day there were more of them.

* * *

Mother's gentleness with people is wonderful. In Kakinada I remember there was a ten year old boy who used to sell vegetables and fruit. The boy loved Mother and used to say he brought his wares specially for Her. Although She often did not need what he brought, She would buy everything he had and give him extra money to make him happy.

There was an old man too in Kakinada who used to catch snakes and play with them. He used to visit Mother and delight in telling Her stories of catching the snakes. Sometimes he would play with them before Her. The Mother gave him food and money: whenever the old man needed either, he knew he could come to Mother and ask Her.

Mother's hospitality and generosity are great, as anyone who has ever stayed in Her house in Germany can witness.

* * *

I have observed that Mother and Nature are in close harmony. In 1985 Mother had to have Her wisdom tooth out. The day before the operation was clear, but on the day the doctor took out the tooth there was rain and terrible wind. Nearly always when Mother is ill there are clouds or rain and snow. Nature is in intimate sympathy with the Mother and laughs and grieves with Her.

Another way in which the Mother demonstrates this harmony with Nature is in gardening. She is a devoted, wise and tender gardener. She takes as much care of plants as She does of human beings and animals.

With Her care I have noticed flowers and fruits are happy and yield enormously. In 1984 a single carrot grew with several large heads. Once one rose plant had sixty-five roses and a bean pod grew fifty centimeters long. Once also the hibiscus plant was flowering well; Mother praised it and it blossomed even more. People often stop and admire the beauty and order of Mother's garden.

Mother is aware of all the plants and knows exactly what each needs. She gives them individual care. Some are given frames; some fertilizers; for some She makes supports out of branches. I have noticed that when She waters plants She does so with great delicacy, as if they were newborn children. Whenever a plant is ill Mother nurses it carefully. Sometimes She gives it medicine; sometimes She encourages it by talking gently to it. Once She took out some plants at the side of the house that were ill and gave them a shower in the bath-tub. It was a beautiful scene.

Mother knows exactly what to do in the garden. It is as if the plants themselves tell Her what they need. Once Mother pruned the branches of the fruit tree. A devotee said it was not the right time. Mother smiled. A few weeks later the fruit tree that had been sickly was thriving!

It is inspiring to watch Mother working in the garden. She is so gentle and devoted. Once I picked a fruit roughly. Mother said, "If someone pinched you wouldn't it hurt? You must be delicate with plants. They are very sensitive."

* * *

Mother's cooking is as creative as Her gardening. She is never mechanical; She enjoys discovering new recipes and synthesizing old ones. She also enjoys making East-West mixtures. The food She makes always seems to have a delicious taste. She is happy to cook for people what they like. Sometimes she doesn't even taste what She prepares; She knows instinctively when it is good. Mother herself eats little and has no particular preferences. Her care in preparing delicacies for others though is immense. Her cakes are especially delicious!

Mother is also an excellent seamstress. She makes blouses, frocks, skirts, all to Her own patterns. She prepares Her own designs and embroiders on sarees. Other embroiderers admire Her work.

Mother also works in other ways in the house. During 1986 there were many changes in the house in Thalheim; Mother participated in all of them. She is very efficient with a drill. Devotees who have seen Her working remark that She seems frail but is in fact stronger than any of us. When I met Mother in 1974, there were many things that I knew and She did not. Now She is an expert in many techniques I am ignorant of. At that time, for example, Mother understood only Her own language – Telugu. Now She also speaks and understands Hindi, English, and German.

Her quickness at picking up technical things shows itself again and again in the house. If anything goes wrong She watches carefully how it is repaired and can do it Herself later, when necessary. Mother has an independent, self-reliant nature. She is delighted to accept help but will also go ahead unperturbed without it.

As all devotees who have worked with Mother or watched Her work will witness, Mother has a great capacity for work and great concentration. Technicians think She is a technician; painters a painter; architects an architect. Each imagines Her in their own image. In fact, She has, and transcends, all skills. In everything She does Mother is a perfectionist. She has a great respect for tools, too. From Her the hammer, needle, brush all receive the same honour. They reward this by working harmoniously with Her.

Mother never wastes anything – neither time nor effort nor space. She is extremely practical, clear-minded and commonsensical in all aspects of life.

Every day I am with Her I am more amazed at the range and extent of Her gifts. She shows me and all of us how we should live – with clarity, sensitivity, practical efficiency, kindness and concentration.

Mother's Conversation

Mother speaks little, but beautifully. She is precise in everything She says, and always to the point, without being harsh.

When Mr. Reddy was alive, his love and knowledge of Mother created a fine atmosphere for talk with Her. He would state his feeling on a variety of topics – from politics to yoga – and Mother would give Her opinions. It was to Mr. Reddy that Mother confided the experiences given in this book. Often Mr. Reddy would ask Her about other Saints and Avatars and She would tell him about them.

Once Mr. Reddy asked Her opinion about the family. Her answer is very characteristic of Her. She said: "The family is the root of creation. The world is a big family. If you lead a good family life, you will have success in the Divine life. To be peaceful and loving in the family is as difficult as sadhana, sometimes even more difficult." This shows how down-to-earth Mother is in Her thinking and how much She respects the complexities and dignity of ordinary existence.

In Telugu – Mother's native language – Mother can make delightful jokes. She has a subtle sense of humor. Her jokes are never pointed, however, but always full of kindness and sensitivity. They often show a knowledge of language that is remarkable for someone who had no schooling.

Many people have remarked on the beauty of Mother's voice. Sometimes it is low and gentle, sometimes it is childlike. Its effects are always joyful and calming. She has a lovely, delicate laugh.

Mother has a large range of knowledge and when necessary expresses Herself strongly. She has a fine taste in painting, for example (as well as being a marvellously original painter in Her own right). In our conversations, to find out Her taste in art, I would often show Mother paintings, and She invariably liked best the ones that were most natural, realistic and full of feeling. She appreciates depth and truth of emotion over mere surface brilliance of technique and loves warm and rich colours. Her criticism of art I have found is always concise, logical and analytical. In Italy when we visited the Prince of Thurn and Taxis I saw how clearly She could distinguish the different styles of painting and how much She loved the devotional spirit of the old paintings. Once a devotee showed Her a Chinese landscape painting from the nineteenth century of a tree. Mother remarked that it was not natural. The tree had blossoms only, no buds; all the flowers were open in the same direction and with the same colour. In all things Mother loves a spontaneous and living order.

I have noticed that when Mother answers the questions of devotees it is always with a quiet exactness that satisfies the heart. She says what is needed, with no fuss or rhetoric.

Mother's Nose Operation

On January 29, 1986, Mother went into hospital for a painful operation of Her nose. I would like to give an account of this time because it shows how brave and dignified Mother is under the impact of physical suffering. Her fortitude and patience during this time were very moving. I myself was distraught; it was an anguish to see Mother in pain. But Mother even in this condition was at peace. Mother went into the operation room at 11:30. I felt that She left Her body before She was given anaesthesia. I asked Her later. She said that She had.

The operation itself lasted three hours. It was shocking to see Mother after it, unconscious, and with a bandage across Her nose. I almost fainted. Then I had a vision. In it Mother and I were walking down one of the corridors of the hospital as if we were going to visit someone; Mother was in a white sari and smiling. This vision put my heart and mind at rest. After the operation Mother was taken to a cold room where She shivered terribly. Although She was unconscious, Mother replied exactly to questions I asked Her. When She awoke She remembered nothing of what She had said except that She had been cold.

After an hour, Mother was brought to our room. I asked Her if She was in pain. "A little," She replied bravely. That same evening devotees visited Her. They were struck by the atmosphere of peace in the room. Naturally, it was very sad for them to see Mother in this condition.

Mother and I stayed in the hospital for a week. In that time the hospital staff became very attached to Her. They did not know who She was but they responded to Her great gentleness.

During that week devotees used to come and see Mother. Even in Her weak condition, Mother gave advice and helped some of the devotees with their health problems. One of them remarked that Mother looked beautiful even when ill. Sometimes when the doctors wanted to examine Her nose Mother refused, like a small child afraid of pain.

Her fear was justified, as proved by what happened over a week later when the time came for the doctor to remove the bandage across Her nose. He did so without warning Mother of the pain that it would cause Her, and very roughly. Mother fainted. It was a terrible shock. Her whole body was covered with sweat, Her clothes were soaked. I called continuously to Her to wake up but there was no reply. After fifteen minutes She became conscious again. All the doctor could say was that this pain was usual; even boxers, in his experience, had not been able to stand it. Part of the sacrifice a Divine Incarnation makes is the acceptance of such pain in the body. It is very humbling to think of a love so great.

Mother's convalescent period was very hard for me. I felt Mr. Reddy's absence acutely. Mother was clear and strong throughout and sometimes very sweetly childlike. Her dignity even in such an ordeal is an inspiration for us all.

Mother's Grace and Power

When we were in India there was a great panic all over the world about Skylab; some people, frightened that the satellite would fall on land asked Mother to save the situation. Mother visualized Skylab's movements and willed that it should fall into the sea.

Once an American professor came to the Mother and asked Her to save his friend, a prominent leader of India, Lok Nayak, who was on his deathbed. Mother agreed and said that the man would live a little longer. Then the announcement came on the news that the Prime Minister had announced Nayak's death in parliament. The announcement was due to false information. When Mother was told about Nayak's death She said it was not true: She saw Nayak living. Then a second announcement came that Nayak was alive. Mother then said that he would not survive long as his body could not sustain life much longer.

It is important always to remember that Mother's help is not bound by time or space. A devotee wrote from Paris and said that it was difficult for him and his family to come and visit Mother in Germany for financial reasons, but asked Mother's blessings for his family. Later he wrote to the Mother thanking Her for saving the life of his daughter. She had been drowning and cried out, "Mother Meera save me," and was saved.

A devotee wrote from France who had seen Mother's photo. He prayed and asked the Mother to help him to solve his money problems. The very next day he bought a lottery ticket and won: his money problems were solved. Then he prayed to the Mother for a job: the following day, he got it.

Recently a devotee's mother was in hospital suffering from cancer. The devotee asked Mother to save his mother. Mother assented. The operation took place. The doctors had no hope. But the woman got much better.

In India there was a car accident and the victim, on the verge of death, was given some powder that the Mother had blessed. He is still alive.

Once in Germany Mother was telephoned and told that a devotee's baby was in the hospital in critical condition. The doctors had no hope. The parents asked the Mother to help the baby. The Mother assented and immediately started to sweat in Her body and tremble and shiver. Mother was plainly taking the anxiety of the parents and the pain of the baby into Herself. The baby was saved.

Mother's generosity to Her devotees is unbounded. Ever since She was a child She wanted to have a house where She could receive guests. Now, in Thalheim She has one. Everything is done to ensure the comfort and happiness of the devotees who visit Her. One devotee said, "The wonderful thing about staying with Mother is how free She makes you feel. Her love is unconditional and this reflects itself in the way you feel at home in Her house."

In many other ways also Mother shows how tenderly the Divine in Her human form responds to the love of the devotee. For instance, Mother was invited to Duino Castle by the Prince of Thurn and Taxis in June 1985. Mother does not like to travel but because of the Prince's devotion to Her She went. It was wonderful to see how naturally Mother moved in such regal surroundings. How like a queen She seemed in those days!

The Prince told Mother of a friend of his who was in extreme mental suffering because he thought he had a fatal disease. Mother asked if this friend had actually been checked-up medically, adding that he was not ill but should go to a doctor immediately and see for himself. The friend went to the doctor's the next day; in fact he had no symptoms whatsoever of the disease he thought he was suffering from. He came to Mother with tears of gratitude in his eyes.

Mother visited the Prince of Thurn and Taxis again in November 1985. The Prince was dying and She wanted to show Her compassion. When we arrived the Prince was very sick and only truly conscious when talking to Mother. Her kindness to the Prince is an example of how Mother will go to great personal lengths to make a devotee happy.

Recently, at Mr. Reddy's request and as a special sign of love for Her devotees, Mother gave a Darshan at midnight on the New Year. Devotees especially love this as the New Year can then begin in Mother's presence and with Her blessing.

Mr. Reddy
November 1979, Canada

MR. REDDY: THE DIVINE MESSENGER

*"There is nothing else I want from
this life or any other than to be
with Her and do Her work and be of
what use to Her I can."*

Mr. Reddy

Balgur Venkat Reddy was a rishi, a great saint and a divine messenger. He was a conscious soul. From his childhood he had a clear vision of what he desired.

When he was young he cried and cried for months continually for "Mother". His human mother was with him, but she could not satisfy all his inner needs. At that time it happened that he read a book about Saradamayi, wife of Sri Ramakrishna. While reading it, tears rolled down his face continuously, it moved him so much. Thirst for "Mother" went on increasing. He didn't usually read any kind of book, and it was the first time he read a book and cried so much. It was his psyche crying. He didn't only cry at the first reading of the book, but whenever he read it, even many years later.

During that time he used to see Mother Meera's face very clearly, and wanted to meet Her. Because of this, whenever he saw a person who resembled Her a little, he was a friend to her. He always searched for the Mother in women. His whole and only aim in life was to find his real Mother. For that he sacrificed his life, family, society, name, fame and finally realized his life purpose as a divine messenger.

It was Mr. Reddy who introduced to the world the Divine Mother Meera, the Avatar of the New Age. We cannot think of Mother without Venkat Reddy, nor of him without Mother. They are interrelated and interconnected. Many times I observed that what Mother felt and thought, he reflected by his thoughts, feelings and actions. He was a portion of the Mother. She was completed by him; he was a part and parcel of Her. In some respects he was a father, brother, and even a mother to Her. He looked after Her sometimes as though She were a child. At the beginning She really was a child to him, and he took the whole responsibility of the Mother on his shoulders. He is an ideal model to everyone who wants to surrender to the Divine in each of his actions, thoughts and feelings, always connected and concentrated towards the Mother.

Mr. Reddy was deeply sensitive to Mother. He appreciated the beauty of the Divine in Her actions and thoughts, and observed Her movements and followed Her in a way that never inconvenienced Her. Even during his illness he always asked me about Mother: "Did She take food in time? Did She have enough rest? How is Her health? Is She alone or does somebody accompany Her?" He worried about every little detail. When he was healthy he wanted to tell the whole world, "Here is the Divine Mother. Turn towards Mother. If we knock at the door the Divine will open it, and it is the hour of the Divine Mother. So awaken and find Her. She is here before us." He wanted to tell the whole world about the Divine Mother's presence, so that mankind might be conscious of Her, and be transformed.

When he became ill in 1981, Mr. Reddy completely withdrew from the outer world. He had no longer any taste for publicity about the Mother. He knew that slowly and gradually the time was approaching when the Mother would be known to the world by Her silent action. During these years, his outward movements were limited. He rarely spoke to anybody. Day and night he did japa (calling of the divine name). If he talked, he talked about Mother and with Mother. Even during the talks, he used to ask about Her welfare and actions.

Sometimes he was a child to Mother, and sometimes he disagreed with Her and argued with Her like a child. But when She said to him, "Don't do it," or "Don't eat it," he followed wholeheartedly what She told him. The relation between Mother and Mr. Reddy was very sweet. Each was in certain ways dependent on the other. If something happened to Mr. Reddy, immediately Mother felt it. And if Mother was sad, at once he felt it very clearly, and sometimes he told Her the reason for Her sadness without himself knowing what had happened to Her. He consoled Mother; She got much comfort from him. Here we can see how the devotee can console the Divine with pure devotion like a child.

Naturally, Mother also looked after him with much care and love and affection. Here one can see how the divine love flows like a stream: sometimes Her love flowed boundlessly. During his illness Mother's only concentration was on Her loving child. And Her child's concern and love was only for Her. For Mr. Reddy, Mother was all. He used to recite from the Bhagavad Gita: "You are my mother, father, brother, sister, and everything to me. Without You there is nothing. I cannot exist without You." These words are the truth; what he said he practiced and followed.

For Mr. Reddy, sadhana was not a hard tapasya, but a play with the Divine Mother. Our every action, thought and feeling can be connected and offered to the Divine. Only then can we realize the Divine. Mr. Reddy was always thinking about the Mother and always acting and feeling according to Her will and wish. Mr. Reddy surrendered to Mother: Mother also surrendered to him. Ancient Indian scriptures say that the Divine is bound to the devotee. Mr. Reddy gave himself totally to the Mother. He often said, "I used to search for the Mother outside, but now She is within – in my heart." Many times he asked Mother and requested Her that when he left his body She should keep him in Her Golden Temple Heart and never leave him alone even for a fraction of a second. His only wish was to be with Mother in Eternity.

I met Mr. Reddy in 1969 in the Sri Aurobindo Ashram. He helped me. He always helped the people who came to the Ashram with deep aspiration for the Divine, whoever they were. With this intention he saved many who wanted to commit suicide. He consoled them and showed then the right path that leads to the Divine. He was doing karma yoga without expecting anything from the people whom he helped. He said he looked back on his whole life as a preparation to meet Mother Meera.

In his adolescence Mr. Reddy was socially minded, and wanted to reform society. When he was sixteen he started a boarding hostel for about a hundred fellow students. The chief of police of Hyderabad at that time was Raj Bahadur Venkatrama Reddy. He was the founder of Reddy College and several hostels and educational institutions. Venkat Reddy was still a schoolboy but wanted to start a hostel by himself. He collected some donations and went to the chief of police for his advice. At first Venkatrama Reddy thought he had come for a donation and was surprised to be told that only his advice was wanted and the money for the hostel had already been collected. The chief of police was impressed with the young Mr. Reddy and asked him to accompany him in his car and gave him every help and advice. He also instructed his officers to help in any way they were asked.

Mr. Reddy was a leader of men from his childhood onward. He respected others and they respected him. He never looked down on others, whatever their state might be and lived harmoniously with everyone. He was serious and strict in nature, but at the same time loving. He loved dignity and discipline. He never cared for himself, and to help others he often neglected himself. In spite of any difficulties he was always happy and joyful. People used to ask him how he could always be so happy. He used to reply that he was content but did not know from where the joy came. He was like a spring of joy. He was not religious, neither an atheist nor a theist, but a man of intuition and inspiration.

In his twenties, Mr. Reddy married. As he was socially minded, he dedicated himself to the cause of Vinobha, a close associate of Gandhi. Vinobha was like a friend to Mr. Reddy and Mr. Reddy worked with him wholeheartedly. Vinobha used to call him "Mother" because Mr. Reddy took care of him and others who were in need with such loving attentiveness. He loved them in fact like a mother. Ramakrishna told his disciples, "The Mother aspect is essential to the human being whether male or female. Through it one can easily find God."

During this period with Vinobha Mr. Reddy would sleep only four hours a day. He would wake up early in the morning and accompany Vinobha on his walk from village to village for the "Bhoodan" tour (asking landowners to give plots of land to those without it). He used to walk 30 or 40 kilometers a day sometimes without food or water. Very little rest was taken as there was so much work to do. This continued for months on end, always with only four hours of sleep a night. During these travels, he would give lectures to people with land to convince them to give to the poor. Often, land was given.

A little incident from these days shows Mr. Reddy's gift for diplomacy. There was an old sadhu of Punjab, Sakori Baba, who was the head of a Math (ashram) in Hyderabad. He was like a father to Mr. Reddy. When Mr. Reddy was with Vinobha on his tour near Hyderabad, Sakori Baba wanted to meet Vinobha. Vinobha only accepted food that was personally grown; Sakori Baba wanted to give him a fig. Mr. Reddy told Vinobha that the Baba had watered the plant. Vinobha asked the Baba how he could have done so since he was so old. Mr. Reddy answered for him and said that the Baba used to wash his hands and bathe near the tree. So he satisfied and harmonized both people. All burst into laughter.

Mr. Reddy had the gift of friendship. Wherever he went he was friendly to everyone. He numbered among his personal friends not only Divine Personalities but also politicians who respected his gift of oratory and his passion for truth. Many political leaders visited Vinobha. Mr. Reddy was humble and a kind of personal secretary to Vinobha. Sometimes the President of India himself and other governors of the different states would visit. Mr. Reddy was always cooperative with them, respected them and was respected by them. He was never proud and never wanted power so it was easy for him to be simple as a sage.

Mr. Reddy was a true sannyasi. He married and had no attachment for his family. He had power and money, but no interest in them. Once, he started an ashram in Manchirala in South India. A great deal of money came into his hands. He was not attached to it but spent it carefully.

During this time, Mr. Reddy went to see a yogini Mannikyamma. She lived on the top of a hill where no food or water could get to her. She has not in fact taken food or water for many decades. To visit her you had to go on foot. Once Mr. Reddy meditated with this Mother for twelve hours continuously without a break; he said it felt like a second and that he had no thirst or hunger. Mannikyamma liked Mr. Reddy very much and asked him to stay with her. He said however that it was not his place. Afterwards he met another Mother, Chinnamma. Even after he had started staying with Chinnamma he would visit Mannikyamma. He also introduced many political leaders to the yogini. Nowadays, the place he visited is completely changed; it has become a place of pilgrimage and there is every facility to stay there.

Mr. Reddy continually attracted holy people by the force of his sincerity. He loved Ramana Maharshi and visited his Ashram many times and he had many friends. He met Sathya Sai Baba in 1960, in the coconut garden in Puttaparthi. Sadhu Subramanyam, Sarvodaya leader of Andhra Pradesh, told Mr. Reddy that he was full of love and asked him to stay with him in Vijayawada. Mr. Reddy also met Ramananda yogi in Andhra Pradesh who is a friend of Sadhu Subramanyam. Ramananda had the power to stop breathing and remain in samadhi many days on end. Once doctors came and tested his heart. It was still and he stayed one week in this condition underground. When he came out he was in good health. When Mr. Reddy told me about his meeting with them, I told him that both Ramananda yogi and Sadhu Subramanyam had been invited to our house and stayed with us when I was a child at school. Mr. Reddy also met another swami connected with my childhood – Ramalinga swami, in Erped Ashram. This swami used to come and stay with my uncle who was his devotee. He used to come in summer because Madanapalle – where I was born – is a hill station and is cool in the summer.

Mr. Reddy was not however happy in Vinobha's work because he was haunted by his quest for the unknown. He was like a madman for some months. During this time he used to sing songs of Bhakta Meera. He liked Meera's bhajans (devotional songs) very much. He sang the song as a mantra to find out the guru he actually wanted. This condition was so painful, so he left Vinobha.

Through the help of a friend, Mr. Reddy met Chinnamma (an avadhuta). On seeing her he felt great relief and understood the Bhagavad Gita and the Vedas. At first sight of her he received wisdom. He said afterwards that his past painful condition was a preparation for the silent mind. With this he understood Chinnamma. Here he quenched his thirst with divine knowledge. At that moment he decided to spend his whole life at the feet of Chinnamma. She told him that only the company of Adiparashakti would be right for him. He said later that after being in the company of Mother Meera he received what Chinnamma told him.

At that time he wrote many letters to friends and acquaintances about Chinnamma. He was a great letter-writer. His letters touched the hearts of the readers, and many came and saw Chinnamma. Mr. Reddy wanted to spread the word about Chinnamma throughout India. Once there was a religious meeting in Madras. He wanted to talk about her in that meeting and went to Madras. There he met a man from Pondicherry who was attracted to Mr. Reddy and told him about Sweet Mother and invited him to Pondicherry. In Pondicherry Mr. Reddy met Sweet Mother and later went to live in the Sri Aurobindo Ashram with his family. In 1956 Sweet Mother gave them permission to stay in the ashram permanently.

During his stay in the ashram, Mr. Reddy used to go to the samadhi at 5:00 in the morning until 7:30. He meditated near the samadhi. Then in the evening from 5:00 p.m. to 7:00 p.m. he again meditated there. From 1956 until 1972 that was his daily program. Many times during his meditation he saw a golden sun so brightly that he felt the sun's rays were on his forehead. Thinking it was the sun he would open his eyes

Mr. Reddy merging with the Divine Mother
June 21, 1985

and find to his surprise that there was no sun so early in the morning. He had many great experiences and realizations.

Once during meditation he saw Shiva (the Destroyer) sitting under a tree meditating. He heard the voice of Shiva saying, "Silence and meditation." Once more he saw Shiva telling him, "Bachelor life is very pure." He had always given importance to brahmacharya, and he put it into practice. He used to say that it helped him in his life to keep him in good condition. When he was young he read about brahmacharya and was impressed. So he decided to practice it wholeheartedly throughout his life. Once he felt that he was in a big hall, where many avadhutas (realized souls) were sitting in rows waiting for food. He served them food and went away. But two dogs followed him. He gave them food also and they became avadhutas. Then he realized that God is in all.

During meditation once he saw Sri Krishna. He was very fond of Sri Krishna, and had a strong desire to hear his flute. On this occasion Sri Krishna asked him to listen to his flute. He prepared to hear it, but when Krishna started to play Mr. Reddy went into trance. Then Sri Krishna merged into him. This happened many times.

Mr. Reddy longed to hear Sri Aurobindo's voice. Sri Aurobindo came to him as he was meditating and began reading his poems. When Mr. Reddy heard his voice, again, in the same way, he went into trance. This also happened many times. Sri Aurobindo asked him whether he heard his poems; Mr. Reddy could only reply that whenever he started to listen he went into trance, so he could not hear it. Sri Aurobindo smiled and merged into Mr. Reddy. After this experience Mr. Reddy realized that we cannot hear the Divine Voice with this normal mind. Only with the higher and illumined mind and in silence can we perceive the Divine.

Mr. Reddy said that with Chinnamma and Sweet Mother his life and his sadhana had been a preparatory stage to find the Divine Mother Meera. In July 1972, he went to his village, Chandepalle, and there in his own house he saw Mother Meera. He suddenly felt that She was Adiparashakti, and remembered what Chinnamma had told him, that the right place for him was with Adiparashakti. At once he decided to be with this Mother. At that time She was a child and unknown to the world as Divine Mother. He remembered the face which he used to see forty years before. Mr. Reddy had always had a strong wish in his youth to take care of a small child from his village and show her to the world in such a way that the whole world would respect that child. When he was young it was his greatest longing, but he didn't know how it would be fulfilled. When he saw Mother Meera, when he met Her in his house, it was clear to him and he was very happy.

In 1973 Mr. Reddy left the ashram permanently and returned to the village and took the responsibility for the Mother. For this he had to sacrifice his family, and his only daughter whom he loved dearly. That is to say, he left his attachment for his daughter. He had a clear vision and intuition about his love for his daughter. Twenty years before he had thought clearly that if there was any world for him it was in her. If he lost her, then there would be no relation to the world left. His vision came true after twenty years. He said many times that he lost the world and found the Divine. He became empty so the Divine could fill him with Her Love.

During his stay with the Mother, She revealed many divine secrets to him. Day and night he vigilantly took care of Her without caring for himself, the family, society or the world. So after a while the time came when Mother took complete care of him. He totally gave himself up to Mother. From 1981 to 1985 Mother took complete charge of him. From time to time the Mother dictated Her experiences to Mr. Reddy and he wrote them down. The Divine Mother told Her divine secrets to nobody in the whole world except Mr. Reddy. This shows how great and noble he was and how much trust the Divine had in him. Many times the Mother woke him up in the middle of the night to narrate Her experiences. He wrote them at once while She told them. He was always alert even during his sleep. He always slept consciously, and many times when he woke in the middle of the night his eyes shone as if in the daytime.

At the end of 1981 Mr. Reddy was very ill. The doctors had no hope. But the Mother silently worked on him and he came to life again. Day and night She looked after him with full care and love. He was in the hospital for six months. His mental and physical condition were not good at that time. The Mother was encouraging him to take food, was Herself feeding him; She was scrupulous about his health. At this time She stayed in the hospital late hours in the night caring for him. Under Her sensitive care he regained his hopes and love for living only for the Mother. His mental and physical condition became better.

At this time the Mother declared openly to him and those near them that he was a Special Being who had come for a special purpose. His physical ailment made him withdraw from the world, go within, and towards the Mother. He had no more outer relationships. He went to the hospital regularly for dialysis and came back home and stayed with the Mother. Now and then, if any disciple of the Mother came and held conversation with him, it was about the Mother.

During these five years there was a rapid inner development in Mr. Reddy. All the parts of his being – mental, vital and physical – were concentrated on the Mother alone. His only wish was that after his departure he would be in the Golden Temple of the Mother. He wanted to be united with Her. During this period, throughout the day and night, he did japa and meditation constantly and continuously in the Presence of the Divine. Even though he was suffering from various diseases, his face looked fresh and shining. He looked like a young man, and never like an old person.

Whenever the Mother called Mr. Reddy by his pet name "Gundu" (complete and round), he smiled like a sweet child and answered Her affectionately. When he was angry at the Mother, he cried loudly, calling Her and telling Her what he wanted. Then the Mother consoled him by patting him on his back and sometimes kissing him on his forehead. This cooled him down quickly. It was beautiful to see him as a child of five or six years who quarrelled with his Mother and would not speak to Her. But he wanted the Mother to come and console and talk to him. When after some time She talked to him, he burst into tears and wiped them with his hands and asked Her why She had not come sooner. Here we can see the loving nature of the Mother and the child. Sometimes She wiped away his tears and tickled him. Then he laughed and laughed, and when it became unbearable he begged the Mother to stop tickling him. Then tears of laughter rolled down his face. This is a wonderful Leela of the Mother. Here we can feel the love of the Mother flowing towards Her child.

Afterwards he asked Her to pardon him for his ignorance and asked Her never to leave him under any circumstances in this life even for a short time or even after his departure from his body. Once he asked the Mother, after his departure from this life, to keep his body for three or four days and do with it whatever She liked, either put it into the ground or burn it. Even his body he gave to Her to decide what to do with it. He didn't keep any wish for himself. He gave himself completely to the Divine. All his wants, wishes, and aspirations were fulfilled.

For nearly two months before his departure he said the days were not passing, they were lingering, moving very slowly. During this period he had no taste for anything, his only taste was for the Mother. Day and night his love for and attachment to the Mother were increasing tremendously. He sometimes thought that it would be better to stop dialysis, which he felt separated him from the Mother. Before he entered the hospital, the last day, that is, Tuesday June 11, 1985, he listened to all his favorite devotional songs of India, and he rejoiced in the devotion of the devotees, how they surrendered their lives to the Divine, how they gave up the ego and the self to the Divine. Afterwards the Mother fed him with Her hands and took him to his bed.

The very next day, Wednesday June 12, 1985, he went to the hospital and stayed there until the end. During these days he was in intensive care, and during all this time his body was shining, until June 17. On this day the Mother smelled a special fragrance emanating from his body, similar to the perfume emanating after his departure. On June 19, 1985, the Mother worked in Her garden, pulling out the weeds from it, concentrating the whole time on Mr. Reddy, as if She wanted to make the way clear for him to Heaven. Physically, She dug out the weeds from the garden, which meant that if at all there were any difficulties or any disturbances for his long journey, She was making the path clear and clean so he could travel easily. She took off all that was unwanted and made a clean and clear path to the Garden of Heaven. On that day the Mother felt clearly that his body was now like that of an ordinary human being. She noticed that his lips were closed, and She felt that they were closed forever. At that time his heart and blood pressure were in good condition. The Mother said that during all these days his body had been shining, but today there was nothing special about it. As soon as She saw it She felt giddiness and Her whole being was full of sorrow. Afterwards She said that on that same day Mr. Reddy had left us all alone.

On June 20, 1985, we went to see him in the hospital. The doctors said that he was a great man, and they said that he had told them a week before his departure, during dialysis, that he saw many beautiful flowers in the Garden of Heaven. By talking of this wonderful garden, he had bidden them farewell. Mr. Reddy used to say to us that he never spoke anything about the Mother or about himself in the hospital. But the people there felt that he was a great man, and so they respected him. The doctors told us that he was conscious about his departure.

On the night of June 20, 1985, Mr. Reddy came to the Mother like a big cloud, and there were many small clouds with him. He brought all the small clouds into the Mother's room. He came first and merged into Mother Durga. Afterwards all the small clouds were also merged into Mother Durga.

As Mr. Reddy was a part of the Mother, when he left his body the Mother felt that some part of Her was divided from within Her. This feeling was too painful to be expressed in words. As we know, the Mother had never done any painting. But this pain brought Her to paint the relationship of Mr. Reddy with Her as a Divine Mother. We can feel Her sorrow in these paintings. They are full of feeling. We can see and feel Her love towards him. A German artist said on seeing the paintings, "This is real art. It is a revelation of Divine Love. These are masterpieces. The composition, colour combination and the technique are marvellous." We could watch Her hand when She was painting and could immediately see how the master hand controlled the brush and colour. She painted directly without making any sketch. Her hand moved freely and easily according to Her feelings. During these days, after Mr. Reddy's departure, each day She painted one picture, according to Her experience.

On June 23 at four o'clock in the morning, Mr. Reddy's soul came to the Mother and began pouring continuously his whole being into Her. The process took half an hour. On June 24 he came and slept by the side of the Mother. She patted him and asked him to wake up. But he didn't; he said he had to sleep, so he never awoke again. On that day we went to the cemetery at 12:00 noon to see his body, but the casket had already been closed, and we did not see his face again.

I always feel Mr. Reddy is with us. His departure was a very distressing experience for the Mother. During these days She was like the Mother of Sorrows of the Universe. I saw and felt whenever I touched Her, that sorrow was flowing from Her like a river. After he left, for many days regularly at 4:00 p.m. the Mother had severe pain in the heart. This pain remained for three to four hours. At that time She looked mad with sorrow. There were many great changes in Her body. For some days She had a strange feeling in the stomach and whenever She lowered Her head it seemed as though all Her organs were coming out of Her mouth. There was a vomiting sensation. She was giddy, and when She walked She felt as though She was flying in the air. At this time the Mother looked as if She were somewhere where we could not reach Her. Her face was filled with sorrow.

After his departure, many times Mr. Reddy was with the Mother throughout the day and night. The presence and powerful love of Mr. Reddy has stayed with Mother and myself. Death has not separated him from us.

On June 19, 1985, Mother saw Mr. Reddy in a cowshed. There was a large tub there filled with water for the animals to drink from. Mr. Reddy was sitting on its rim. His white dhoti was hoisted around his waist because his knees and legs were in the mud. Mother explained the mud symbolizes the earth. Mr. Reddy wanted to come to earth.

Mr. Reddy was with Mother from July 19, 1985, until 10:00 o'clock on the morning of July 20. He told Mother he slept and closed his eyes in the way in which he had left his body. He said, "Now I am well and free from pain."

On July 25, Mother was working on Mr. Reddy's samadhi, levelling the earth. Suddenly She saw there was a boil on Her hand. She continued to work nonetheless. The boil burst and filled Her palm with a burning feeling. Mr. Reddy told Mother that his body was also burning in the same way.

When Mr. Reddy was in the body, I often used to ask him what to do if I had a problem. He always advised me well. One day in 1986 I was looking all over the house for something and could not find it. I was exhausted. Then I thought of Mr. Reddy and asked him where it could be. He answered me gently that it was in the corner. And there it was! I was struck with wonder. He answered me as though he were in the room.

When Mother was having Her nose operation in early 1986, Mother and I were in a double room in the hospital. I smelled the fragrance of Mr. Reddy very strongly when the Mother came out of Her cold room to the one we shared. Every day in the morning I smelled the same fragrance.

If ever a problem arises I think of Mr. Reddy. Sometimes I dream of him, and he is always loving and consoling. His beautiful character is very fresh in my heart. He helped me deeply when I was in the Sri Aurobindo Ashram and it was through him I came to work and stay with the Mother. Mr. Reddy is still helping me in more ways than I can explain.

One of the Mother's devotees who had loved Mr. Reddy came to see the Mother after four years of being away. He told the Mother that he felt the presence of Mr. Reddy very powerfully in the house. "Yes," Mother replied, smiling. "He is here. Only his body is not."

* * *

From the SRIMAD BHAGAVATAM

(p. 44, 45. Translated by Swami Prabhavananda)

Our senses, O Mother, draw us to things, because we love the world. If we direct our love toward God we find divine knowledge and absolute freedom. But there are souls who find such great joy in love and in service of the Lord that they have no concern for their own salvation. Even so, divine love ultimately brings freedom to them also.

Those who love God as dearly as themselves; those who have affection for Him as for their children; those who trust Him as their beloved companion, and revere Him as the teacher of all teachers, those who love Him as their friend, and worship Him as the highest – theirs is eternal life.

Blessed indeed are they that steadfastly devote themselves to the worship of God, for they shall attain absolute freedom.

"...They love Me and meditate on Me in order to realize the highest good. When the heart becomes calm, and the mind becomes united in Me through Love, then is attained the Supreme Good."

From letters to Mother about Mr. Reddy

"On Thursday, June 29, I was with my young friends when Andjela phoned me that Mr. Reddy had left his body. One part of us is sorrowful; we liked this sweet man very much, this adorable grandfather; the other part is silent before this great moment. His departure has indeed a very deep spiritual meaning, a meaning of course we are unable to understand.

We send you and Mother our love; we can imagine your affliction, even if Mother and you know a lot more than we do, that all is not finished for Mr. Reddy. A Mahatma's death is not the end of his work."

* * *

"A few weeks ago, while meditating, spontaneously I called Mr. Reddy inwardly. And there was a great warmth... This call to Mr. Reddy was my spontaneous call in the sense that it was real and somehow tangible, and felt physical. Whenever I meditate I do the japa OM NAMO BHAGAVATE MATA MEERA, but there has been no connection with the heart: I realized that the call to You has been mental and that it has prevented me from grasping Your truth entirely. When I was a child I used to watch saying that what I would really like is for God truly to exist and for me to work for Him. It was during that call to Mr. Reddy that a spark of that Reality dawned on me, was felt concretely, even if for a few seconds. There was great warmth and tenderness."

* * *

"It was Mr. Reddy who brought us to You and taught us, by his example, how to worship You in Your majesty and love, in Your great and inexhaustible tenderness. His love for You and Your love for Him helped us to understand something of the sublime mystery of the love between the Divine and the devotee. His body has left us but his spirit is closer to us than ever, as an inspiration, as a guide. Now we who are left must be worthy of his trust in us."

Mr. Reddy and Mother Meera. India 1978

QUESTIONS AND ANSWERS

When we have Your Darshan, Mother, we do pranam in front of You and You take our heads between Your hands: What are You doing?

On the back of the human being is a white line running up from the toes to the head. In fact, two lines start from the toes, rise along the legs, join at the base of the spine and then become a single line reaching to the top of the head.

This line is thinner than a hair, and has some knots in it here and there which Divine Personalities help to undo. It is very delicate work and great care has to be taken to undo the knots, as there is danger for your life if the thread is broken. When I hold your head then I am untying these knots. I am also removing other kinds of obstacles to your sadhana.

When I touch your head, the light moves upwards in the white line. It indicates, like a meter, the development of your sadhana. When there is no progress, the light moves downwards along the line, showing the degree to which your sadhana has deteriorated. When the light is continuous from the toes to the top of the head, the person may have many experiences and visions, although some people have visions and experiences without this white line. When the line gets to the top of the head, people have the Paramatman Darshan. When the line has gone above the head, then there is a constant relation with Paramatman.

If your aspiration weakens, the line moves downwards as I said. One day you might even fall from your sadhana. This is a great crisis, which can however be prevented. In front of the body are two red lines starting from the toes, growing gradually upwards on either side of the legs and tending to meet at the base of the spine where the white lines become a single one. If the red lines reach the white line, you will achieve absolute detachment. This rarely happens and only to those who have the divine shakti.

By the growth of the white and red line the sadhana will be established permanently without possibility of a fall. If the red lines develop fully, you will reach great heights. The white lines will also help to support the experiences of those who have a psychic opening. Even when there is a psychic opening there is still the possibility that it will close. The opening of the psychic is effective for sadhana, but it is not enough. The establishment of the white and red lines will help you to keep the psychic continually open. If the psychic can be compared to a flower, the lines are the plant itself.

When we have done pranam we look into Your eyes in silence: What are You doing?

I am looking into every corner of your being. I am looking at everything within you to see where I can help, where I can give healing and power. At the same time I am giving light to every part of your being, I am opening every part of yourself to light. When you are open you will feel and see this clearly.

Should we follow gurus?

It depends on the guru. In exceptional circumstances, a guru might be necessary, even vital for spiritual development. Generally it is best to pray to the Supreme directly, or approach Him through one of His Divine Incarnations. That is more useful. If any human guru is giving you teachings that bring you closer in your heart to the Divine, listen and be grateful and follow them. But be clear about the limitations of all human gurus. They can only point the way; they cannot take you there. If you want to see the Divine, why don't you ask Him directly?

What daily discipline helps us realize the Divine?

Remember the Divine in everything you do. If you have time, meditate. Offer everything to the Divine. Everything good or bad, pure or impure. This is the best and quickest way.

What is the best technique of meditation?

There are so many techniques. Generally they confuse people. Quite often they increase people's spiritual pride instead of destroying it. You have to be very careful. The best way is to remember the Divine in everything and to offer everything to the Divine.

Do I have to leave my job and family to do Your work?

No. Sadhana can be done within family life. People should stay where they are and turn all their attention to the Divine and open to the Light. That is all and is everything. You don't have to be near me physically to do Yoga. Wherever you are, if your aspiration is sincere, I shall be with you.

Can I reach the Divine through art or work?

Don't go to the Divine "through" anything... go directly. Realize yourself and see that everything you do is filled with light. Don't live for your work only; live for Him and do your work in Him and for Him. If you surrender to Him truly, it will no longer be you who does the work but Him who does it through you. You will become a channel for His power and His will and His light. This takes time and a great purity of heart and motive.

What attitude should I have towards my spiritual experiences?

Be grateful. Offer them to Him, but never think of yourself as special or chosen. That leads to pride, and a proud man is far from God: Whatever experience you have had, however extraordinary, remember that there are further and greater experiences. The Divine Life is endless; the being of God is infinite. Remember the aim of our yoga is not experience, not individual illumination, but the transformation of the whole life, a continual experience of Him, an unbroken ecstasy. And be careful always; there are so many ways in which the vital and mental can imitate and pervert the spiritual. In ordinary consciousness, in which most people are, it is hard to tell where an experience comes from. The best attitude is wariness and humility. Rest nowhere and become attached to nothing – even your own deepest knowledge.

Mother, why do You speak so little these days about Your experiences?

People can do nothing for my work until they themselves are realized. So all energy should go into that work of realization. What is the use of telling people things they cannot understand until they are realized? It might confuse them; it might make them vain or proud. What I want is complete simplicity and complete surrender, not words, not discussions, but action.

I believe in Jesus. Must I stop believing in Him and believe in You?

Whomever you believe in, believe with all your heart. All Divine Incarnations are equal. Be sincere, open, and my help will be given to you always.

What should I ask You for?

Ask for everything. Everything. Do not stop at peace of mind or purity of heart or surrender. Demand everything. Don't be satisfied with anything less than everything. Our Yoga is the transformation of human life into Divine Life here on earth; it is a hard Yoga and it demands those who have the courage to demand everything, to bear everything and to ask for everything. God wants to give you everything – have the courage to ask for the humility to accept everything. You have my help always.

What is the Paramatman Light like?

It has every colour in it and the colour and the force of every light of every plane. It is everywhere and in everything.

What is the importance of the Paramatman Light?

I called down the Paramatman Light. The Paramatman Light is in everything. The work of transformation will be done much more quickly, providing people are open. Even if they are not open now, the pressure and power of the Light are so great that they will become open.

What should my attitude be towards sexuality?

The work is done fastest and most purely if you can live without sex and beyond desire. But very few manage that and for many it is extremely dangerous to try to transcend sexuality before they are ready. What is essential is not to renounce it, but to offer it.

Do You feel any special attachment to any country?

Wherever there is aspiration, I will feel happy. My work is not for one country or one race or one people only; it is for the world.

I am afraid, Mother, that when people come to see You they interfere with Your work. Is that true?

Nothing can and nothing will interfere with my work. If the whole world came to me, my work would not be interrupted or deflected for a moment. I am working on all planes. I am working everywhere. This earth is only one of the planes where I am working. How could anything disturb my work?

How do we receive the Light and what do we feel when we receive it?

People receive it in many ways. Some receive it through the head, some through the fingers... what do details matter? It is the effect that matters. What are its effects? An unmistakable and extraordinary lightness and happiness and peace. The Supramental Light can burn slightly when you receive it: the Supreme Light does not hurt. You can receive the Light anywhere and at any time. Knowing that, open to it without delay. There is no time to waste.

What should my attitude be towards politics?

Pray to Him that there should be peace. Bring down Light into your life so that you can do His work of peace in the world. Understand that the pain of the world will only be healed when the world is transformed in God and work with all your heart and being that it should be accomplished. Do not be distracted by anything from that work.

What is my past life?

Forget the past. Live in the present and remember the Divine.

I read in a book that one can realize the Divine within an hour.

With Divine grace one can realize the Divine within a second.

Once a disciple brought some special stones and asked Mother if they would help him in his spiritual development.

If you believe that God is in the stone, then it helps you in your sadhana.

Is it necessary to awaken the kundalini?

When the Light descends in the body it is not necessary.

Mother, may I know Your work, please?

First of all, I bring down the Light and establish Peace, also I help the people to surrender to the Divine, to remember the Divine and to be faithful and sincere to their religion or to their belief. I help people to be happy in their families.

When someone asks for Your help You simply say "Yes". How do You help them?

There are different Lights which serve different purposes. I send whichever Light is needed.

Who am I?

Give up the "I" and you will know.

SOME TESTIMONIES BY DEVOTEES

1. ADILAKSHMI OLATI

I live with Mother Meera and I hope I shall always live with Her and within Her. I graduated with an M.A. in philosophy from Sri Venkateswara University of Thirupati and at the age of twenty-five I suddenly left home and family to look for God. I just got on a train and came to Pondicherry, and after some time I was accepted by Sweet Mother into the Ashram. That is putting it very simply, but why take time here to explain everything?

The first time I went to the Samadhi of Sri Aurobindo I saw Him; He embraced me and comforted me. I knew nothing about Him but I saw Him and I saw too that He had a fractured leg. It was very clear. Every day when I meditated at that time I used to see a kind of film of *Savitri*. It just projected before me. And Sri Aurobindo used to say in my vision, "Now go and look up page so and so, line so and so." And what I read conformed exactly with what I had seen. Sweet Mother accepted me into the Ashram in 1969. I stayed until 1980. I have left that now to give everything to Mother Meera. I say "give everything" but in fact it is Mother Meera who is giving; I am receiving, just by being with Her all day as I am, painting or sewing or cooking... and I am fulfilled. I cannot put it any other way. Everything that I have ever wanted is here with Mother Meera. I feel no anxiety, no distress. What should I say? This is what I have wanted all my life.

Once, long before I met Mother Meera, I had a dream about teaching Sweet Mother Telugu and She had difficulty in pronouncing the letter and sound "illa". Isn't it strange – when I taught Mother Meera Telugu it was that same letter She found hard to pronounce! And there is another experience I had which shows me very clearly who Mother Meera is. Long before Sweet Mother left Her body I dreamt that we were together upstairs in Her room. She came out and gave me Her Darshan. Suddenly She jumped down from upstairs and disappeared. I searched for Her everywhere. Then I too jumped from the same place to look for Her. Even though I jumped from very high up I wasn't hurt at all. When I landed I saw a little Mother sitting, and a great light was coming from a small star-like mark on Her nose. I understood that anyone would recognize the next Mother from that star on Her nose (many disciples were around Her). Even though Her form was different, I saw that it was the same Mother. I want to tell you that the first time I saw Mother

Meera She had the same star-like mark on Her nose, but I didn't connect it with the dream until later. I have no doubt whatsoever, Mother Meera is the Divine Mother.

When did I meet Mother Meera? In February of 1974, when She came to my house with Mr. Reddy. I had heard Her name before that and felt no reason, that I can explain, why She was very close to my heart. My love started before I met Her just by hearing Her name. Soon after I met Her I decided to offer everything I had to Her. It was as simple as that. I knew She was spiritually great. I felt great love for this well-dressed and beautiful girl (the first time I saw Her I was very surprised that She was so smart and beautiful). I had always wanted to give myself entirely, so I decided to offer Her everything. At that time Mother was staying with Mr. Reddy in Pondicherry. Every day we would see each other and go to the Ashram.

Even though She was fourteen, She had the wisdom and presence of mind of a wise old woman. And Her work was perfect, nothing was ever wrong with it. She worked calmly and thoroughly on everything She did – washing or cleaning or sewing or painting – just as She does now. And She was so kind to others. She would never miss an opportunity to do something for someone else. Then and now She loves to make people happy more than anything. Sacrifice is always part of Her nature. Such perception, such wit, and such clarity in all that She says! Her conversations and answers to questions always reflect the needs of the individual. She continues to amaze me even though we have been close all this time.

The first experience I received from Mother Meera was a simple one. It happened soon after we met. I was teaching in the Ashram at that time and everywhere I went I saw Her face. I didn't ever feel that with Sweet Mother, although I loved Her very much and was devoted to Her. Mother Meera's face everywhere... It was extraordinary, never to lose sight of Her face... I knew that I had not been wrong in thinking of Her as special.

I met Mother Meera again in 1976. When I saw Her She was wearing a blue dress and I saw Her as Krishna. People see Mother in the many different forms of the Divine such as Durga, Sri Aurobindo, even as the Virgin sometimes. She is all Divine Forms and all Divine Forms are Her. That day I saw Her as Krishna. It was so simple. There She was in Her blue dress and She was Krishna. It was one of the greatest experiences I had had up to that time, and I loved Her so much for it. It is surprising perhaps to have known Her as being Divine and yet not feel afraid whatsoever. I wonder at Her and I am awed by Her, but I am never afraid. She is so loving. If I don't see Her, I get intensely unhappy. In 1980, I spent four months away from Mother. I realized then that I could not live without Her. I lost 20 kilos, I had no more interest in anything...

There are so many experiences with Her that I could tell you about. In 1978, I saw Sweet Mother's face in a dream. It disappeared and Mother Meera's face came in its place. I understood. Once I was reading *Savitri* in the Ashram Art Gallery and Mother Meera appeared in front of me. I saw Her with open eyes, She was in pure white light – and She said, "I will explain all of *Savitri* to you if you like. Don't worry if you can't understand it now," and then disappeared. In February 1979, just before the strike in the Ashram and the riots in Pondicherry, I was working in the Art Gallery... I saw with open eyes Mother dancing in the gallery. As She danced She changed into Kali, frightening and terrible. How She danced, so wildly! I saw Her with my open eyes! And soon after there was all that violence, those riots.

I would very much rather talk about Mother Meera than about myself. My past no longer exists for me. Perhaps I know Her in an earthly way better than anyone else, I am very aware of how secretive She is, how hidden from our knowledge. She is becoming, I think, more and more secretive, more and more withdrawn. Not unloving, never that, but profoundly detached, not cold but absorbed in Her work. I feel Her remoteness and Her dignity even when She is laughing or cutting vegetables or sitting out on the verandah talking. Her Divinity is in everything She does, and living with Her has deepened, not lessened, my wonder for Her.

If I had to stress one aspect of Her character above all others it would be Her love of truth. How She dislikes exaggeration! How She dislikes hysteria or self-pity or falsity of any kind! She has not a trace of any of them in Herself and She dislikes deeply any signs of them in others. The qualities She likes are frankness and openness, above all. She has nothing to do with the proud or the vain or the complaining. When one realizes what She has been through on the subtle and higher planes... there is no suffering She has not endured and nothing has stopped Her or diverted Her for a moment from Her work; and She is so subtle, too! She never does anything showily. She is equal and patient in everything. She always knows what to do and when to do it – Her timing is perfect. She always knows what gesture to make to assure you of Her love and to comfort you quietly; She always knows what to say to encourage you. When someone is tired, She always thinks of something they need, to make them happy. I never feel lonely or downhearted with Her. Whatever She says She means absolutely. That has given us all who live around Her such joy and calm. I feel so slow beside Her sometimes – She thinks so immediately and so fast it's hard for a human being to keep up with Her. And She knows so much even on a practical plane! Once, in Canada, we were all worrying about some detail of how a washing-machine worked. She solved it immediately! And the building that's going on in this house... well, the architect designed it all one way and Mother said, "No, do it this way it will be better." And he did it, and it was. Her perception of character, even in an ordinary way, is very precise. She sees immediately and knows.

I would like to go on and on talking about Her, but I have said enough. What I have learnt about Her and from Her cannot be put into words. One thing I will say I have learnt – that when we give ourselves truly to the Divine we are not giving anything really, but we are getting everything.

2. BADARINATH OLATI

I met Mr. Reddy in 1969 in Pondicherry, when I was studying Agriculture. He was of a very lovable nature and used to help people on the spiritual path and liked only to be in spiritual companionship. Wherever he was, he tried to make the environment harmonious. He liked to hear about Divine Personalities and talked about them with very great interest. He was a good host, and liked to offer food to others and enjoyed it when people ate food with him. His hospitality towards those who were seeking the Divine was always beyond his means.

It was difficult to get Sweet Mother's Darshan at that time, but through Mr. Reddy I got permission. This was my introduction on the spiritual path. He was very happy if people entered the spiritual path.

In 1978 at Pondicherry, in the early hours of February 21, I saw a young woman with Mr. Reddy and my sister Adilakshmi. On first seeing her, I felt from the bottom of my heart that She was a Divine Person. With my physical eyes I saw white, luminous, soft light around Her body. It was a rare experience for me. I could not put it into words. I did not know who She was and at that time I did not say anything either

Mr. Reddy   Mother   Adilakshmi
Autumn 1979, Canada

to Mr. Reddy or to my sister. Later I came to know that She was Mother Meera.

In 1979, I saw Mother Meera giving Darshan to the devotees. I was very happy to have the Darshan in the company of Mr. Reddy and my sister. I enjoyed the Divine Presence and my heart wept when I had to return to my town, as if I were a child going away from his beloved Mother. Whenever I asked Mother Meera's permission to leave for my home town, I saw Her in dazzling golden light. Even after reaching my town, after a twelve hour journey I felt like a bird flying in the sky. I experienced this almost every time.

Mr. Reddy used to tell me that I could visit Mother Meera at any time. I am forever grateful for his open invitation. He used to treat the devotees of Mother Meera with more love than his own family members.

Like an innocent child, Mr. Reddy would request his Mother Meera to give Darshan to devotees although they had come without appointments. Mother would accept Her child's request. He was very enthusiastic if people visited Mother Meera and happy that they were in divine contact. He used to tell them about Mother; Her experiences and Her Divinity. He used to say that the only happiness in his life was to stay near Her and Her divinity. He was like a bhakta singing the glory of his beloved God. Whenever he talked about Mother Meera, one could see how his face gleamed with joy and happiness. When he remembered the early days when he found Her, and how all their difficulties were over, he used to weep.

His heart was soft; whenever people confided their difficulties to him he used to identify with their sorrows and tears rolled down his cheeks. He consoled and gave the right advice to people in need.

He was a dignified gentleman and of royal nature. He used to say that for the sake of Mother Meera and Her work, he was ready to do anything.

Many times, in the presence of Mother Meera, he seemed like a child of 4 or 5, calling his "Amma" and asking Her something. One could not feel his age at that time. Sometimes, when Mother was angry with him, he cried like a small baby. I felt that he sometimes had the voice and behavior of a small child.

He was a fine letter writer. His letters touched hearts. I used to get letters from him telling me about Mother Meera. In 1981, Mother was in Germany and he wrote me that Mother might stay permanently in Germany. At that time Mother visited Germany for a short time. One and a half year later, She settled in Germany.

After Mother Meera's second foreign tour in 1981, I could not visit Her. I heard of Her only through letters. My heart was longing to see Her. In June 1983, I came to live with Mother Meera. Naturally, my joy knew no bounds. I felt as if I was in Heaven. This experience lasted many months. When I saw Mr. Reddy in Germany, he was a dialysis patient. He could hardly walk by himself, his eyesight was poor, his worldly relations were almost finished. But he was in the careful protection of Mother. In Mother's presence you could not tell that he was a patient unless you were informed about it. He said that he wanted Mother and nothing else because he had found Her after many years of search and difficulty. He was totally surrendered to Mother.

He said that whenever Mother assisted him in walking or any other work, he felt he was safe and could completely rely on Her. He was happy that he was under divine care and protection. His adoration for Mother was very great and he was always conscious of respecting and loving Her.

Soon after knowing Mother Meera, I had a strong urge to live near Mother Meera's divine presence, but I did not express my wish externally. One day, one of the devotees asked Mother about his wish to live near Her. The Mother replied that at an appropriate time his wish would be fulfilled. So I took Her reply as an answer for my inner urge, and my urge was fulfilled at a later time, with Her Grace.

Mr. Reddy's love, care, respect, and attention were enormous towards Mother Meera. No human being was as attached to Her as Mr. Reddy. Mother was everything for him. I think he showed us how a true child should be in the path with the Mother. Though I am small in every aspect, I pray to Mother with all my heart to prepare me in Her divine path and help me to proceed in the footsteps of Mr. Reddy.

3.

First Moments

One day, as I was asking
Mother if She had a proper symbol,
She answered She had none to Her
knowledge and added: "Is the joy
in your hearts not sufficient as a
symbol?"

I had been staying at the Sri Aurobindo Ashram in Pondicherry for nearly six months when I heard, around July 1978, of an eighteen year old girl from a rural region of Andhra Pradesh who was in contact with Mother and Sri Aurobindo and who was seeing them constantly. I was extremely astonished by this announcement. In the following months I tried to get more information on this young girl. I was told that She had been in Pondicherry but left. Thoughts about this mysterious young person were constantly on my mind, in an obsessive way. Finally, in September or in October, I cannot recall for certain, during a meeting I obtained a few typewritten sheets of questions asked of Meera (as She was called at the time) by a few personalities of the Ashram. Meera's answers astonished me. Then, I asked Mother and Sri Aurobindo to tell me who was Meera and if it would be useful for my yogic development if I met Her.

The following night, I saw two Sri Aurobindo symbols, the first one of modest dimension in proportion to another great one, both of opaline shade. In the center of the largest one (where one usually sees the lotus in the center) I saw, majestically seated, a woman with a child on her lap, like a Madonna and child. At the right and left of these Divine Beings I saw a few people in a posture of adoration. My heart was filled with love. When I woke up, I could not explain this strange vision. At this time, in the middle of October, I became more conscious that something was going on (already since August inexplicable changes were perceived). I was curiously shaken. Days went by. I knew inwardly that important things were happening.

On October 13, a friend with whom I was often conversing about Meera (because it had become the sole subject that I could talk about), told me that a resident of Auroville already knew Meera, that She was in Pondicherry, and that he would take her to Meera at five o'clock. Next morning, I went to my friend, impatient to know her impressions and obtain Meera's address. My friend said that she had been quite moved to meet Her.

Immediately, I went to the given address. A man welcomed me courteously (it was Mr. Reddy). I asked to see Meera. He talked in a strong voice in Telugu and I heard, coming from a room, a voice of unforgettable tone, lingering, as if it was coming from a profound ecstasy. It was my first impression of Mother.

Mr. Venkat Reddy said that Meera was giving me an appointment at five o'clock in the afternoon. On that day, the celebration of Mahakali (October 31, 1978), I feverishly awaited five o'clock. Earlier by intuition, I had bought three incense sticks; one labelled Meera, the other Durga (because I had learned from the question and answer sheets that She was in contact with Durga) and another "Eternal Smile". I arrived at five o'clock; I was announced and with a beating heart I waited. Meera entered dressed in a blue sari. I handed Her the incense sticks. She looked at me, then said to Adilakshmi (the admirable woman who attends and serves Her) that She already knew me (Adilakshmi translated). I asked Her several questions concerning my health problems and my work, and She answered with assurance, poise and an infallible precision. From this first meeting, in an inexplicable way, I named Her inwardly Eternal Mother, and repeated these words constantly while She was looking at me with an extraordinary intensity. I remained with Her half an hour the first time.

When I came out, I had the absolute conviction of having met the Divine Mother in a body. I went to the Samadhi of Mother and Sri Aurobindo praying to them to undeceive me if I had made an error. But I was assured of being in truth. Once I took *Savitri* and asked Sri Aurobindo to tell me who was Meera. I pointed to a page with a papercutter; it fell on the passage starting with, "Madonna of Light, Mother of Joy and Peace..." (Book seven, canto 4) that ended with, "One day I shall return, His hands in mine, / And thou shalt see the face of the Absolute. / Then shall the holy marriage be achieved, / Then shall the divine family be born. / There shall be light and peace in all the worlds."

The following days and months were the happiest in my life. I introduced Her to a few friends. Every day we learned new facts about our adorable eighteen-year-old Mother; every day before our eyes She became more and more the Queen of the Worlds. There was no place for anything else in my life but this extraordinary revelation. Around Her, the atmosphere was always charged with intensity and I could feel Her Light accompanying me everywhere. In a short time She made me progress more than I ever imagined, and I was made deeply content with Her gifts. That state of delight remained till May when the personal difficulties started to appear. Then I had a series of painful months. But Her Grace always accompanied me and made me overcome the obstacles that are inevitable, it seems, on this path. I constantly feel Her Help, Her Protection. I thank Mother and Sri Aurobindo for this ineffable and glorious coming of Mother Meera on this earth for the completion of the Work. I am Her child always.

October 7, 1980

With Mother Meera in Germany

I had the extreme happiness, from February 9 to 18, 1984, to stay near our Mother Meera. She lives in Thalheim, a village situated in the neighbourhood of Limburg (nearly 90 kilometers from Frankfurt). It is a hilly region, wooded with coniferous trees, that recalls the Laurentiens in French Canada, with pointed gables in a foggy sky. Mother Meera has made Her home in one of those villages where an impeccable order prevails.

What inexpressible joy to find myself near Her and to bathe in Her presence. Never before had I felt Her love so strongly: it is this aspect of Her that impressed me the most during this brief stay. Inwardly, I keep Her glance and Her smile, the marvellous moments of intimacy in Her physical presence. I had not seen the Mother in two years; it seemed as if a change had been accomplished in Her, and that all Her being was emanating more Softness, Compassion, Love than before (if that is conceivable). I thought that such growth was a result of the descent of Divine Love experienced in April and May 1983. Never had I seen Her in such inexpressible Beauty (not evident in the photographs of Her, although the Power is present). Near the Mother, we constantly feel the intensity of the Divine Presence, under diverse Aspects. Sometimes one is dominant – the Love vibrations, or overwhelming Peace that leaves you speechless, or the Almighty Light – at other times, a young and fresh joy. What emanates from Her, what She gives us, is always different, according to the circumstances. The whole house of the Mother is filled with the Presence; even in the village, and all the surroundings, Her presence is directly felt. About half-way between Frankfurt and Thalheim, I felt that I was entering Her atmosphere. I had the impression of a white Light similar to the one known at the Sri Aurobindo Ashram in Pondicherry.

What a great joy it was to see Mr. Reddy and Adilakshmi, for whom I have a profound gratitude, as well as a respectful friendship. Adilakshmi is, as always, full of concern, energy, joy and fervor to serve the Mother.

We all know that Mr. Reddy was seriously sick and hospitalized for six months on his arrival in Germany. The doctors had declared that he had few weeks to live, but the Grace of the Mother saved him. He was transformed inwardly through his sickness. He lived entirely detached of everything, filled with the Mother, united to Her. We talked a great deal, and his words of fire were of a great spiritual seeker who, after many ordeals, found bliss in his identification with the incarnate Supreme Mother. All his conversations were related to Her and he communicated ceaselessly his desire to be consciously united to Mother Meera and be enlightened by Her. What else could have any value than this Enlightenment at the end of the path, this blissful fusion in the beloved Mother.

Now it is possible to converse directly to Mother in English without any translator. We can talk intimately; Mother asks our opinion on this or that; everything She does, She does with complete simplicity. Still, we can perceive that Mother bathes constantly in a Divine Glory and that Her Power is unlimited.

The mingling of simplicity and sublimity imposes on us discretion in matters that are beyond our comprehension: a modesty prevents us (except under exceptional occasions, for some needs) from asking questions to the Mother on higher planes, on Her condition, on Her work, on the future of the world, etc., as if we have a feeling of a misplaced curiosity; besides, we feel such an intense Peace and Joy near Her that it does not come to our mind to try to penetrate the secrets of the Mother. All mental curiosity is abolished. With the Mother, no more questions. Only the evidence of Light. Once, I permitted myself to ask Her, because it is in the mind of many, if the physical body transformation could be accomplished in a short-term basis. She answered that, "It could take time," without more precision. Through Mr. Reddy, I learned that the work of the divine Light infusion was rapidly being done in all the planes of manifestation, even down to the most dark and material. Therefore, we submit to the Mother occasionally, problems in our personal sadhana (spiritual work) or ask Her advice concerning questions on our external life, our family, or friends, etc. She always answers willingly. From Her answers, or in a conversation, it happens that we may catch a glimpse of the infinite depth of Her knowledge and Her way of being. Disturbing obliteration of the One who is invested with Shakti, the Supreme Mother descended to accomplish the universal Transformation...

It was with reluctance that I left Mother, and these blessed days were very short. But I know that we can live constantly in Mother, and make in Her our home, in repeating Her name, by appeal, by aspiration, and by the surrender of ourselves... Mother often mentioned during my stay that what is most important is japa or inward repetition – as much as our activities permit it – of the name of the Divine Personality in whom we trust. Amma Meera (this is how I call Her – Amma means Mother in Telugu – which is also the first cry of all infants) Amma Meera answers to all demands, especially if we know how to have the heart of a child being trustful in his Mother.

March 30, 1984

Near Mother Meera

Again this year, from February 4 to 13, I had the joy of visiting Mother Meera in Germany. Since that stay, I try to keep alive the treasure of the marvellous Love emanating from Her. Her physical Presence, indeed, makes us particularly conscious of Her Love aspect.

The private conversations with the Mother unfolded (directly in English) in the most perfect simplicity and tenderness. I was able to express directly my personal preoccupations (life, family, sadhana) and ask Her advice and help.

From Friday to Monday Mother gives Darshans. I was amazed, the first evening of my stay; in walking into the meditation room before the coming of the Mother, I received a sudden mass of Peace like I had never previously felt.

Whether during Darshan or personal meetings, the presence of the Mother bathes us – many of us felt it – in an extraordinary Divine intensity (of Peace, of Joy, of Light, of Love and of Power); the experience of Her contact always appears different.

The face of the Mother seems still more radiant than before, the eyes and the smile always revealing with more strength and magnificence Her almighty eternal Love.

I would like to obtain news of Her experiences and Her present work, but on those subjects Mother has great reserve.

The state of health of Mr. Reddy demands three dialysis per week. His physical condition has brought him to a constant inwardness. He speaks little, and we feel he is immersed in the Divine, in a state of contemplation.

Mother lives in a village in a beautiful valley, wooded with coniferous trees. Every day, I took walks and could again realize that the region was impregnated with the infinitely soft and luminous atmosphere of the Mother.

May we have the capacity by the japa (the repetition of Her name) to live always no matter where we are in the marvellous Presence of Mother Meera in us and around us.

April 1985

Departure of the Messenger of Mother Meera

In the beginning of June, Mother Meera made a brief stay in Italy, invited by a disciple living near Trieste. I went to meet the Mother. Those days of fullness, but overshadowed at times by news, on the telephone, about the state of health of Mr. Reddy, the protector and collaborator of Mother Meera since 12 years. He had to stay in Thalheim because of his need of three dialyses weekly and his extreme weakness.

I accompanied the Mother and Adilakshmi to Germany. The health of Mr. Reddy had deteriorated since my last visit in February. The Mother and Adilakshmi were sitting with him in the living room. He was so weak that his head rolled like one of a new-born baby. Nevertheless, he seemed profoundly absorbed in a superior consciousness.

The dialyses that previously were not difficult became, in the last weeks, very painful and provoked a kind of disequilibrium in his organism. He confided in the German disciple in charge of accompanying him to the hospital for his dialysis, that it was as if each cell was suffering. One day, when few disciples were near the Mother in the living room, he suddenly said in a low voice: "I am full of pain." This small sentence was so pathetic and revealed something of the immense sacrifice that the great messenger of the Divine assumed to bring about Mother Meera's Work of Transformation. It is a deep mystery of the soul, how he endured such a heavy burden in the name of love and compassion. At the center of Mr. Reddy's existence was an ardent will to help others. The carrier of a blazing universal love, he could reveal the supreme importance of Mother Meera's Incarnation for the world. To this new Avatar he surrendered all his strength till his final years which were filled with many great ordeals.

One morning not long before Mr. Reddy was hospitalized, I was telling Mother a story and was surprised that he could follow the plot, when suddenly, he intervened with a keen reflection of the action of the Divine in the world. His reflection showed how acute his perception had became of the constant rising of Grace in the play of the world, and of the warm compassion of the Divine. Even though his body was pained, his consciousness was crystal clear.

The final words that I heard from him were so sweet, having come from the depths of his soul.

On June 12, he was admitted at the hospital after his dialysis. The Mother visited him twice a day. Mr. Reddy was in intensive care; it was hardly possible to stay more than ten minutes each visit. The Mother Herself informed the doctors about the condition of Mr. Reddy. They said that the rate of sugar in his body had suddenly become very high. Afterwards, they discovered an infection which required antibiotic treatments. The first days the Mother talked to Mr. Reddy and he could answer. She undertook Herself to feed him as long as possible. Then, a tube was placed in his mouth to withdraw secretions; another tube in his nose to give him oxygen. He always stayed peaceful; a luminosity spread from his body. We saw on the face of the Mother an unaccustomed gravity.

On Sunday June 16, many German disciples – with the Mother, Adilakshmi and Badarinath Olati – went to see Mr. Reddy. On that day, he appeared transfigured. He radiated a mysterious beatitude. His whole being expressed a noble beauty and a supernatural strength. At that moment, I am certain, Mr. Reddy knew very high states of experiences. When I saw him before I left, I could not rediscover the same expression of majestic beatitude. Later on the Mother told me that on this last visit (on the 18th) the consciousness had departed from his body.

I returned to Italy on the 18th; two days later, The Mother telephoned telling us about his departure.

Mr. Reddy will always remain for us a model of submission and fidelity to the Mother, of love and childlike ardor to serve the divine Work. He knew the infinite joy of living near the incarnated Mother, but also the struggle and suffering in the accomplishment of the mission. Mr. Reddy came on earth to permit the descent of Mother Meera among us. The intense need that he had of the Divine Mother and his devotion for Her called Mother Meera. His role was then to recognize Her and to give Her his constant care. He had for Mother Meera an infinite love. Many times towards the end of the life of Mr. Reddy, the Mother affirmed, in Her discrete manner and without any emphasis, that "he was not an ordinary human being". He was a Divine Emanation to promote the universal evolution.

In the invisible, I am sure that Mr. Reddy – beyond the continuation of his own spiritual growth – pursues actively the action started for Mother Meera and Her Work of Divinisation of mankind and the universe.

To this great messenger of the Divine goes our gratitude for all he has suffered and accomplished when he was in his physical body.

August 15, 1985

Towards You, Mother, climbs my humble gratitude for the wave of Benediction, of Grace, of Love that I feel surrounding and penetrating me. I know that You are always with me and You make everything possible for me. I am Your child and I belong to You forever. Thank You for all that You have accomplished for my parents and friends, for the world. May I live in such a perfect intimacy with You that I merge in Your Presence: live in me and may I live in You forever.

October 1986

Mother Meera and Adilakshmi
Thalheim, Germany 1995

Mother Meera
Supreme Shakti,
turn our beings
integrally, totally
towards You.

Mother Meera,
may Your Grace
preserve us forever
in the glory
of Your omnipotent and eternal Love.

Mother Meera,
may we become forever
One with Your Heart.

Mother Meera
may, by Your Grace,
each vibration, each cell
of our beings
serve You perfectly
day and night.

Mother Meera,
make us integrally, totally
conscious of You,
That we may never want
anything else
than being You, Your Will.

Mother Meera
Supreme Ananda
Supreme Consciousness
Supreme Reality.

4.

On the day of my 26th birthday November 16, 1979, I met Mother Meera, Mr. B. Venkat Reddy, and Adilakshmi. From the beginning I never separated them; from the beginning, for me they were one.

This non-differentiation expresses itself in the following sentences. The Creator creating as the creation – Mother Meera, Adilakshmi and Mr. Reddy. A sense of differentiation is present, but in my heart and in the realm of my intuitive speculations, they are One.

A Brief Note about Myself

I was not raised in a religious spirit. Until the age of 8, I grew up in a socialist country, and the first thing I thought was: "God does not exist. God is a man-made product."

It is interesting to note that many values inculcated by this system proved to be, later on, an immense treasure for me on the path of Cetana-Yoga. But, until the age of 26, I considered God as a philosophical concept, as an anthropomorphic creation. The notion of the sacred was awakened in me in Marocco, where I lived for ten years. The feelings of reverence were not associated with God, they were associated with Art.

For as long as I can remember, I was inhabited by a yearning, by an élan towards beauty, by a longing to transcend everyday life, by a longing to merge into something higher. But this higher did not have a name, nor a form. I called it Art, but not one creation succeeded in erasing the ache of the yearning. By the side of this yearning was emptiness. A dense, almost palpable emptiness. An emptiness almost aware of itself and no longer able nor willing to bear its own state.

The first time I heard the name of Mother Meera, an intolerable and senseless agitation rose in me: intolerable, for never in my life had I experienced a feeling of such intensity; senseless, for I neither knew who Mother Meera was, nor did I have any notions of the concepts "Mother", "Avatar", "Evolution of the manifested Divine in the Matter", etc. This inner agitation was so devastating that I fell ill. I was consumed by high fever. A friend came to visit me, and he brought me a present: *The Adventure of Consciousness* by Satprem. I read the book without intervals.

The next day I attempted to obtain mental silence. I had the following experience. Everything became transfixed, still. Descending from above, and raising from my chest, a white, milky light enveloped me. I was totally bathed in a sweet, warm, milky light. My heart was violent. A spontaneous prayer rose in me. It was the prayer for sincerity. The next evening I went to see Mother.

The First Encounter with The Mother

When I entered the house on Aylmer Street where Mother was staying, my heart began to beat violently, in the same manner as during the experience of the white light.

While waiting for my turn for the pranam-darshan, I thought my chest would explode. When my turn came, my friend (the one who gave me the present, *The Adventure of Consciousness*), introduced me to the Mother. He told Her that it was my birthday and that I was coming for the first time. The Mother nodded. I knelt before Her. She took my head in Her hands. Many times I have tried to remember what happened inside of me at that precious moment, but without a result. All I can remember are the Mother's eyes, the Mother's hands, my friend, and my violent heartbeat.

When I came home, I started to meditate. Without effort the stillness came. But instead of the white light, I heard a great sound. I felt an upheaval inside of me, as if I was about to be turned upside down. But somebody interrupted me in meditation.

On the day of Mr. Reddy's departure, I had a similar experience. The sound was not present in this experience.

About the Inner Agitation

The day after my first encounter with the Mother, I went to see Her during a question and answer period. Mother was seated in Her armchair, Mr. Reddy, smiling, was seated at Her left. Adilakshmi was seated in the front, translating the questions to the Mother. I asked the following question: "Why Mother, did I have this devastating agitation at the pronunciation of Your Name?" The Mother's answer was: "It was the reaction of the anti-divine forces in you, reluctant to change, resisting the Divine Light." (These were not Mother's exact words, I am writing them from recollection.) The following was not said by the Mother, but I clearly remember that this is what I understood from the reply. Without a violent revolt inside of me, I would have never come to meet the Mother. There was no reason for me to come. I did not believe in God. This incomprehensible inner revolt at the mention of the sacred Name, led me to the Light, led me to God.

Many times I wished a purer experience was at the root of my encounter with the Mother, but I guess this experience was necessary to begin the dismantlement of the atheistic barriers in me. I rose to leave and Adilakshmi translated Mother's last words: "The Mother will help you." I looked at Mother Meera. She smiled. The warmth of the white light experience rose inside me. I was totally bathed in the Mother's smile. I don't know if I smiled back, but I felt that each pore of my body was smiling back. If translated into words, I could now say that at that instant I had a glimpse of unconditional, total love. It was the only time I saw the Mother smile. But a few years later, the Mother Meera Society began publishing a first-page bulletin with the Mother's picture printed on it. The first photograph that arrived from Germany was one of the Mother smiling. When I saw it, I had the same experience of the white light warmth, the same intense Joy of total love. I have the greatest difficulty to retain in my consciousness the Reality of the existence of the Mother. By moments, this reality strikes me. It is like a lightning thought, actually a sense of the vibration of the thought. It comes from above the top of the head.

For a fraction of a second, I feel this Reality is alive. But, in me, there is an incapacity to retain this awareness. It is like a vertigo. The memory of these brief states of awareness has three effects:

1. It makes me aware how mechanical, how unconscious, how dream-like my behavior, my feelings and my love for the Mother are in everyday consciousness;

2. It puts me in a state of dissatisfaction, for there is an awareness that all states, all experiences, are incomplete in comparison;

3. It fortifies the will to advance on the path towards the Mother. And since the will is not strong, even after seven years, I have a clear, distinctive feeling that I am far from ready to contain the Grace of True Faith.

My Encounter with the Mother is yet to come. And the One who sustained me and who continues to sustain me on that Path, the One who gave me and continues to give me the necessary strength to continue on that Path is Mr. B. Venkat Reddy.

My Relationship with Mr. B. Venkat Reddy

From the beginning, the closest to my heart was Mr. B. Venkat Reddy. There was such Love, such Devotion, such Serenity in His presence. His eyes, His smile, His posture, and later, His messages in letters, opened a direct passage to my heart. From the beginning He seemed so familiar to me, as if I had always, always known Him.

Mr. B. Venkat Reddy awoke in me a painful tenderness, a mixture of joy and sadness. Sadness came from the awareness that just a part of me, the heart, responded. The rest of the being did not participate. It was not a question of resistance, it was a question of incapacity.

It was through these feelings awakened in me by the presence of Mr. B. Venkat Reddy that I began to understand with every fibre of my being the meaning of my condition as a human being, the meaning of the notions Sacrifice, Free Will, Necessity, and also, the meaning of the necessity for the birth of a new Necessity.

Actually, Mr. B. Venkat Reddy taught me Reconciliation. But I see I am not the best of students, for since the morning of June 10, 1985, I have the greatest difficulty reconciling with Mr. B. Venkat Reddy's departure. It is on this morning, June 20, that I received a phone call from Adilakshmi informing me that Mr. Reddy had left us. I did not cry.

I felt an immense space in my heart, and a sharp pain, a kind of pain I had never felt before in my life. It was a pain of great, great loss, a loss that could not be quantified. And amidst this immense space, amidst the sharp pain of great loss, there was also an unknown feeling until that moment, a feeling that something very grave had occurred, something unpredictable, something that brought to a still centuries of efforts. It was as if, once again, the Great Separation had to occur – not out of Necessity, but for another reason, a reason that transcends me.

It is also on June 20, 1985, in the early morning hours, that I had the following experience. An intense shaking of the body awoke me from sleep. Even if conscious that my body was lying on the bed, I was above it, but I did feel the density of a body around me. This body was shaking, for inside and outside of it, a very rapid current was circulating. In front of me, on the bedroom wall as if on a screen, was the precise picture of my country house and the surrounding countryside. A part of me, at high speed, was flying over this countryside. I do not know how long the experience lasted, but when it stopped, I accidentally noticed that it was 3:19 a.m. At 10 a.m. Adilakshmi called me. She told me that Mr. Reddy departed at that hour. It is true that there is a time of difference between Germany and Canada, but I cannot help but feel that Mr. Reddy communicated something to me.

Three months later I fell very ill. Even if it was physical illness, I knew what was ravaging me inside: I was assailed by doubt. Several times during these seven years I was confronted with doubt, but this doubt was becoming capitulation. I came across a passage in Sweet Mother's Agenda:

> They know what they should do.
> They know what they should not do,
> But they continue to do it.
> Of all the obstacles
> It is mental arrogance
> Which is the most difficult to surmount.

These are the words delivered to Sweet Mother by Kali, during a Kali Puja. (These are not the exact words. I translated them from recollection.)

The reading and assimilation of this passage was the beginning of recovery.

To the prayers for sincerity and peace, I added the prayer for humility, and the following occurrence definitely raised me above this infernal state. I had the following dream. I was with the Mother. I could not see Her. I did not know where we were. I just knew that it was somewhere "high". The Mother was telling me: "Look, you exist on these four planes." From above, I saw myself sleeping in bed, and I saw and felt myself being on four levels. I was observing the four states; they were myself. The Mother added: "You exist on these four levels, but never forget you are always with me."

The process of waking up was a merging with the body sleeping on the bed. The joy, the lightness, the vigor inside me cannot be described. I had inside of me the certainty that nothing, nothing could make me fall again, that nothing could destroy me. And from that moment, each fall was not really a fall, since I did not identify with it. Not only did the

Mother give me the Grace of Her Compassion, but She also gave me the grace to remember Her Grace.

On the same night of my dream, my mother had the following experience. She could not sleep, for she was very worried about me. Suddenly, Mr. Reddy appeared to her. In a very tender voice he told her: "Do not worry any longer; from now on, your daughter will be fine."

My mother never met Mother Meera, Adilakshmi and Mr. Reddy. Only once she had seen a picture of Mr. Reddy. My mother thanked Mr. Reddy, for he had lifted a great weight from her heart. I realized that Mr. Reddy not only cared for me, but he also cared for those close to my heart. My mother's experience reinforced the certainty of indestructibility: I knew that Mr. Reddy was "back". I like to believe that he is my Protector. For me, Mr. Reddy is the One who paved with his body the Great Possibility, the One who defied static laws by Total Surrender.

About Mother Meera's Answers to My Prayers

My first spontaneous prayer to the Mother was the prayer for sincerity. Much later did I understand that my prayer had been answered at once. I realized this when I understood the meaning of sincerity. At the moment the prayer rose in me, the process was installed.

I had come to understand sincerity as being a state of unity of each part of the being, a state of shared aspiration, a state independent of my good will. I have to admit that when the prayer rose I thought that being sincere meant only purity of motivation. To make sure that my prayer was "sincere", I prayed to the Mother to give me the Grace of making my prayer for Sincerity sincere. But, very soon I realized that to be sincere was not what I expected. The process began, and before I realized that this process was the gradual installation of sincerity, I was horrified. For, in my case, the first step was exposure. Not only did I become aware of the motivations behind my motivations, I also became aware of my lack of sincerity, of inner disharmonies, of inner anarchies. I became aware of the immense egoism inhabiting me and that even if I was aware of it, I was its prisoner.

My initial fatal mistake was to identify with the helpless prisoner. It took me quite a long time to realize that the "helpless prisoner" was indulging in his helplessness. Instead of remaining calm, instead of observing, I mortified my spirit. I felt a "fake", for there was such a discrepancy between what I was in the external way of being and what I had discovered inside of me. The closest description of this state is: gates closed for centuries opening at once, and a flow of troubled water rushing out. When I understood that my inner torture was due to indulging the helpless prisoner, in the pride of the helpless prisoner at its ability to sustain so much suffering, I was incapable of feeling mercy for myself, incapable of accepting the deformations, even if deep down I knew that I was swayed in the dark water of the ego, even if I knew that I should make the effort to see, to accept, and to offer to the Mother without interference, without judgements. I knew what I should do, I knew what I should not do, but my mental arrogance prevented me from "being" this knowledge.

It is at that period of confusion, of despair, that the Prayer for peace rose. Several times I wrote to the Mother, asking for Her Help to attain inner peace. Time was passing by and peace did not come. Despair grew, self-blame reached its peak. And then I realized that my letters asking for peace, that my prayers for peace were in reality demands for the pacification of the ego. I remember clearly that when I became aware of this I laughed; I laughed so much, I laughed at how seriously I had prayed. I think that it was the first time in my life I felt compassion for myself.

This interlude of compassion was not sufficient to erase the inner turmoil. But, a great difference in perception was installed: it was as if a fog had been lifted and I came in contact with a cry, a deep need for peace. I wrote to Mother Meera. And my prayer was this cry for peace. At this period, Swami Chidvilasanda, or Guru Mayi, as She is called by Her disciples, was in Montreal. Guru Mayi is the Guru of Siddha Yoga tradition.

I knew that Guru Mayi was in town. Several of my friends were going to see Her and were telling me to come along, but I did not show any desire to do so. The day after posting the letter to Mother Meera with the cry for Peace, I had the following dream. I dreamt that with many people I was entering the Siddha temple. I came in, and was about to take off my shoes as everybody was doing. A man came towards me and told me: "You can keep your shoes on. Your shoes are light."

The next morning, I knew I had to go and see Guru Mayi. I felt a happiness I had not felt since Mother Meera, Adilakshmi and Mr. Reddy

Essen, Germany 1981

were here. When I entered the theater where the ceremonies were held, for the first time in my life I heard the mantra "Om Namah Shivaya". I began singing the mantra automatically, it was so familiar, it was the same feeling, the same love, the same intensity I felt for Mr. Reddy. The song, the mantra, made me feel home.

I sat down, I bowed my head, and I thanked Mother Meera for answering my prayer. I knew that this was the answer to my prayer, that this was the beginning of the quest for peace.

I went to see Guru Mayi every day of Her remaining stay in Montreal. In total it was about ten days. I received Shaktipat from Her.

Through Her teachings, through Her Presence, through almost instant identification with Her during Her Presence, I received a very valuable gift: I understood with every fiber of my being that in order to achieve peace, I had to learn Love. I had to learn the primary thing: Love.

O Mother, how Great Thy Love must be if You are so patient with us.

All that has been written in this section "About Mother Meera's Answers to My Prayers" occurred at Mr. Reddy's departure. Actually, Shaktipat occurred four days after Mr. Reddy's departure. Since the final confrontation, which occurred three months after Mr. Reddy's departure, I am integrating in everyday life the understandings received by Mother Meera's Grace. With each day passing, with each conflict in everyday life, I am trying to incorporate in my thoughts, in my actions, in my heart, surrender to the Mother. I have not yet learned this, but I know that it is coming. I know that by myself I am incapable of doing anything, even incapable of praying. I do not yet feel the Mother's will inside of me, but I do see and recognize my will. And also see and feel that my will no longer wishes to impose itself.

Before reaching the state of total surrender to the Mother, I feel that there is something else that I have to learn. I do not know what it is. I only know that what I have to learn will come from Adilakshmi. I just vaguely feel that it has something to do with synchronicity of heart and action.

Considering that I am a slow learner, it might take some time. But somehow, achieving states does not matter anymore. It seems unimportant. The only thing that matters is that the following Day comes sometimes in space and in time:

May the Day come Mother
When nothing in me wishes to avoid Thee
When nothing in me wishes to hide.

May the Day come Mother
When pure of the Past
I could bow before Thee
With my head high.

Physical Effects

The experience of the White Milk Light occurred on the day upon the completion of reading *The Adventure of Consciousness* by Satprem. It was on the first attempt to obtain mental silence.

I never had this experience again, but from that moment, the following had occurred in consecutive ways.

1. A constant, almost palpable pressure around the top of the head. It did not ache, but it was a vague pain, as the beginning of a headache. When I meditated, or when I did japa, I perceived this pressure as very strong vibrations, something like small white rays. Very often, after the cessation of the vibrations, my head ached.

2. One morning, upon waking up, I heard and felt crackings in my head. Since that moment, I never felt again pain during or after the vibrations.

3. From that moment, the vibrations began to descend from the top of the head, covering the forehead, the eyes, the cheekbones. The vibrations were no longer perceived as separate rays or particles, but it was rather felt and seen as a white milk mass, not as condensed as in the first experience, and not as whole. This gradual descent from the top of the head to the cheekbones lasted several years.

4. Since the experience on the morning of Mr. Reddy's departure and the Shaktipat, the activity is now around the mouth, the tongue and the jaw. As usual, the Force, the vibrations come from above, but, as in the initial first experience of the White Milk Light, from below, from the chest, a force began to rise up. When this occurs, the jaw starts to move

122

very rapidly in both directions. A few times the whole head swayed to the sides, so strong was the energy. Not always, but sometimes, the moments were painful. One day a cracking occurred in the neck. From that moment, I never felt pain again. This energy coming from the chest, is also perceived as white milk light.

5.

Two months before Mother Meera came to Canada, I started to dream about marvellous experiences (She confirmed them after). I was expecting the physical encounter with anxiety. It took place on September 15, 1979, in an auditorium. I was sitting in the first row at the far right, near the side door. The Mother passed in front of me. Mahatma Reddy was preceding Her, and Adilakshmi was following. But I only saw Her. Oh! It was not a burst of Bhakti but a collapse. I was expecting a Greek Goddess and I was only seeing a very simple, young Indian woman. For an hour, opening and closing my eyes, suffering in my body because of the long uncomfortable sitting, my mental was searching for reasons. For an hour, deep inside, I was begging the Mother sitting on Her armchair like a statue, to open me to Her Light. After an hour and a half of personal struggle, I said inwardly: "Mother, I cannot bear this anymore; I give up; do as You wish." I rapidly calmed down. I felt as if I were anaesthetized.

Suddenly I opened my eyes. Mother's eyes were set on me. Physically, Mother was sitting 20 meters away, but Her eyes were only one meter from me. What a look! No words can describe those eyes, both dark and filled up with the whole universe of light. Love was looking at me. A volcano woke up within me; in my bulging chest, red hot lava burned everything in its path, and then time stopped. Alone I would have cried, moaned; I would have crawled to Her feet, I would have wished to die to remain in an eternal ecstasy. I was among a thousand people, so I only let my tears run down, motionless.

Afterwards I heard Mother had looked at me for only a few seconds; but my interior memory can't accept that eternity was so short. I remember a number of minutes.

When leaving the auditorium, Mother passed by me. I bowed to her, trembling with emotion. Then I needed two hours to recover. I had received my great "night of fire".

123

Years went by. Both Mary and Sweet Mother became my "Mothers of Love" again, and I bow to Them with tenderness, but now, Mother Meera is the Mother, The One I'm always calling. Mary was the intangible Light, the sweet invisible Consoler; never did I dare imagine that, some day, I could be gratified with an Apparition, like the one at Fatima or Lourdes, an Apparition just for me.

Sweet Mother was the Incarnation of certainty; the Divine Mother had a body of flesh and blood; I could read Her texts, listen to Her voice or Her music; I even wrote to Her, but I always regret not meeting Her, not serving Her, not receiving Her Darshan. I was sorry to have discovered the existence of the Ashram of Pondicherry too late. I had discovered Sweet Mother only a few years before She left. So I was never sure of behaving according to Her will.

And then came Mother Meera... I could see Her, I could talk to Her, write to Her, I could phone Her, I could receive Her Darshan, and try to serve Her. The Divine Mother is within a body: She accepts to answer back without ever asking for anything, She divinely leads my spiritual evolution. Mother Meera is the outcome of my expedition into the jungle of life: since my birth, in this body and without any doubt in others before, I still have a lot to live through, but Her Divine Hand stretches out to me as soon as danger occurs.

The bhakta and the jnana in me are fulfilled. It is so easy to love Mother Meera that the bhakti is spontaneous; knowledge flows smoothly since I encountered the Source of all knowledge. What does Mother Meera represent to me? I've written a whole book trying to express a small part of this answer of my dazzled being. I will surely write many others.

Mother Meera has granted me rare favours in all fields, even in the physical one. She accepted to help when my body was calling for sickness and disintegration, whereas I was asking for the Divine Light. I just can't tell how much I owe Mother. She has given me so much, but I give Her so little!

My life changed as soon as I understood it was possible to cure a disease by offering Mother the trouble. I'll report some of the circumstances.

When I was younger, I tried all the methods known to stop a hiccup and they worked well. After I became Mother's devotee (1979), none of them worked any more. Then I received intuition: I took Mother's picture and began to do japa. Thirty seconds later, I was cured. Since then, hiccups occurred several times (and they are strong ones), and I always do japa successfully.

From 1985 to 1994, I was often seriously ill. I did a lot of japa. I took Mother's picture in my left hand and a talisman blessed by Mother in my right hand. When the pain was unbearable, I phoned Mother.

In spite of my weakness, I had to give lectures and seminars. Every time, I had to go by car and it took about one hour. When back at home, I was almost unable to walk. Before undressing, I did pranam in front of a large picture of Mother in my bedroom and offered my painful body. Almost systematically my body was quite cured immediately. But sometimes, nothing happened. Now, I know: it is not enough "to offer", the words are nothing. We have to feel strongly, the heart has to be there. A psychic state is necessary, so the Divine Light can work. But this state is not automatic. We can't pretend. We can read that in the Christian scriptures: "In your prayers do not babble as the pagans do, for they think that by using many words they will make themselves heard."

I can't write all the miracles Mother did for me. I will relate only two typical events.

I was very sick and almost unable to sit in a car, but I had to give an important lecture. I went by car to the auditorium after I had offered my body to Mother's Light. As soon as I entered the building, a warm rod settled itself in my body; I was able to walk as a young healthy man.

Technicians had made an error: they had installed microphones for short standing people and I am very tall. I had to give my lecture standing instead of being seated. As soon as I left the public area, I was so weak, a friend had to support me all the way to my car. Mother's Light had made a miracle.

That summer was hot, even in Québec. I woke up one Friday with a burning throat. All day long, my body was exhausted and feverish. Saturday, all the influenza symptoms were increasing. The next night was infernal: I was unable to sleep, the fever was terrifying. In vain, I tried everything I knew. Until Monday morning, my pulse rate was so fast I was almost unable to count it. My head was ready to explode. My heart was tiring and the pain was spreading in my chest. It was very dangerous. I prayed Mother: "Please, be there when I phone you!" Adilakshmi answered the phone. I explained. Mother understood very quickly and Adilakshmi told me: "Nothing bad will happen. The Mother will help you. And you will sleep."

Immediately, I went to my bed and I fell into a deep sleep. One hour later, I woke up. My pulse was normal, no more pain in my chest. It was my first sleep for two days. My body was trembling from exhaustion but the attack was over. Two days later, my body took up again its work. Mother had rubbed out a terrible sickness in a moment, as soon as I was able to receive Her Light in silence.

* * *

Sometimes, Mother sent Her help... and my illness didn't stop. One day, I understood: Grace will move away the fatal danger but I had to learn why my body was sick, and to do what was right to cure it by physical means, not by conventional medical methods which can only rub out unpleasant symptoms. That is true yoga, too.

As I am a writer, all I could find out and practice could be useful to other people, too. At least, I hope so.

I know the key: to offer is to give. If we offer our sickness, the recovery is immediate. If we really give, we cannot, then, give and keep the illness at the same time. It is very tenuous but that is true yoga... and the more I add years to my age, the more I know I am still a beginner in this yoga. Secretly, I hope one day Mother will send me a thunder clap which will split my carapace.

As wrote the French philosopher and scientist Blaise Pascal, we have "to bend the machine" without respite, until the Grace will be allowed to work inside. So, I do japa, hoping a tiny bridge is growing between my usual consciousness and my psychic, so that I can continually love my Mother of Light.

* * *

During a nightmare, I usually repeat a mantra. If I am "connected", the bad experience is blown away; if it's only words, the enemy makes fun of me. I remember a very dark nightmare. All seemed lost for me. Of course, I didn't know I was dreaming. I shut my eyes and thought, "If it's Your Will, Mother, so be it." Immediately, it was a sunny paradise.

All that is easy to explain but it's not at all easy to practice. So, every morning and every evening, during my meditation, I ask Mother to break my carapace and to help me to be conscious.

* * *

Forty years ago, I read at least a thousand books covering health and medical matters. Allopathy, homeopathy, naturopathy, African medicine, Japanese medicine, Chinese medicine, and Ayurvedic medicine interested me. I tried almost everything. What I remember is that nobody knows the real living body. All is beautiful philosophical theory. Every day, I ask Mother to send me the true knowledge. I want to perceive what is going on in my body, to know what to do immediately and to perceive exactly what is the effect of my act. That is true yoga, too. Since I was 22 years old, I knew I was in a body in order to enlighten it and I could not accept to wait for a "specialist" to recite his favourite theory. I was sick in my life, very often, since my childhood. If I had accepted to run to a hospital each time an illness was serious, bit by bit half my body would have been amputated, to say the least. Each time I am very sick, I ask Mother to send me Her Light in order to keep my confidence. She keeps my body alive until I find the true remedy.

* * *

May I add a strange experience?

Mother's pictures are everywhere in my house: I do pranam, I speak to them, and Mother's face changes to express the answer. But, even if my mind knows who is pictured, my eyes don't recognize the true Face. When in front of Mother's physical body, I see Mahasaraswati, the delicate Mother who lays a white rose on a cloud with Her fairy fingers. None of my numerous photos represent *this* Mother. Even if I shut my eyes, I keep on feeling Mahasaraswati. I know it is not enough: Mother Meera is the whole Shakti. My mind can give lectures on this matter but my heart and my eyes don't agree.

I could go on writing hundreds, thousands of pages...

I hope I will live for a long, very long time to serve this radiant Mother, the Sun of my life, the Light expected for so many incarnations. With Mother Meera's help, I hope to stay alive in the same body for three hundred years: it will be necessary to become fully conscious of the Divine. If someday I should leave this body, I only ask one thing: to come back as soon as possible to serve this Eternal Mother again.

6.

In February 1982, after ten years practice of meditation, I saw Mother Meera for the first time. I had an experience of Silence, Rest, and a vision of bright golden Light. Fulfilment and peace were in my heart. Before I met the Mother I painted a face in deep samadhi. I did not know who it was but placed it on my bookshelf. The painting resembles the face of Mother Meera.

At the end of 1982, I had the grace of living in Mother's home. The day Mother gave Her permission to me I saw Mr. Reddy for the first time. I had never seen a man like him before. I had the impression that he was a king, a father and a child. On his face I saw the Light of Divine Love. We were sitting in the Mother's room and Mr. Reddy spoke to us about his search for the Mother, his life in the Ashram in Pondicherry and the time when he found the Mother. I felt at home when I was there. The Mother, Mr. Reddy and Adilakshmi were the Holy Family for me.

The following weeks were full of visions of Light, Fulfilment, Love and Hope. My life was taking a completely new direction. In September 1983 I left Mother's home because I was beginning a new career as a painter. Yet my desire to return to Her home grew greater and greater. I went back in July 1984 on Adilakshmi's birthday.

In 1972, a very large health problem for me had begun. After coming home to Mother I spoke with Her about it. She granted me Her Grace and the problem was cleared up completely by November 1984. I felt the Mother's presence everywhere. I had only to close my eyes to see visions of golden landscapes, golden faces, which I painted. It was at this time that I created my own music also.

In the middle of 1985, Mr. Reddy was in hospital. On the week-end I was in Thalheim and wanted to visit him. I went into the room where he was lying and it looked like a chamber of a king. Mr. Reddy looked like a king himself. A few days later he entered into Mahasamadhi. On the day of his funeral I saw a pillar of light.

Two weeks later, the Mother showed Her first paintings to me. She is an artist. For me, She is the Artist. Her paintings are perfect and

India 1979

powerful, radiant and full of light. For the first time I saw what Art is. Since that day Mother has become my teacher of Art also.

Today, one year later, I am writing this in deep gratitude. My life has changed under the influence of the Mother's love and light. My whole life I have looked for Light, Love and Freedom – now I know a little of what that means.

7.

I met Mother Meera at the same time as a group of other people, through a woman who wanted to lead us on a spiritual path. Things did not turn out the way we had imagined. At times there were confusions and dissensions, important enough to create doubts in my mind. All through one long year I meditated and reflected on the matter to try and find the truth. As I reflected, I realized more and more clearly that my spiritual life had taken an undesirable direction.

Before, I believed that the Divine and myself were separate. Gradually, I understood that we are ONE with the universe; that there is absolute reality on this earth; and that all is in perpetual change. All experiences, good or bad, are there to bring us to spiritual knowledge since it is in the most intense moments that we become conscious. Ever since I started to realize this I have dedicated body and soul to continue my search for truth.

I had the opportunity to observe the Mother during this time. During very difficult moments I could see that She was not "moved". This surprised me. I thought, "It is as if She is watching someone drown and not reacting." My mind was unable to accept these revelations.

As time went by, I noticed great changes in my life and in my inward self. I have always wanted to go right through to the end of suffering to know the truth. During this time I felt I was being put through an initiation. It allowed me to get rid of many difficulties and mental blocks.

Today I am facing new difficulties yet more subtle and much more difficult to overcome, but with all my experiences behind me and with Mother's help, I can affirm that I know I am on the right way. This path from day to day brings comprehension of life and the superior worlds.

What is striking in the way Mother works is that She gives us sufficient energy to break the ego and makes us conscious of our inmost being and does so in harmony with our capacity to support ordeals. What is needed above all is a desire for change and suddenly everything in us and around us will help us towards transformation. But be certain that it will not always be the way we had imagined or hoped for. At the end of the way, however, we will understand that we went through what we needed to go through.

Many spiritual masters recognize different yoga techniques to help their disciples; Mother Meera throws us directly into daily life with all its chores and makes us assume them intensely. There is nothing "spectacular" in this technique, but it has been proved to be very efficient.

Much of my approach I owe, without doubt, to Mr. Reddy. I witnessed his total surrender to the small girl of eighteen that Mother Meera was when She came to Quebec. I could hardly understand how a man of his age could show so much love and give so deeply of himself. I have tried to copy his attitude daily, in offering my life to the Divine. Believe me, it has brought its fruits.

For me, Mother is a precious channel for Divine Energy. Through Her it is transmitted to matter and all receptive beings.

Val D'or, Quebec

8.

On a blessed day of 1979, in the month of October, even the trees in Montreal with their multi-colours welcomed the Mother as if they knew of Her Greatness. From that day on, my life was never the same. In Her physical presence, the mental quiets down, time is crystallized and the whole being bathes in Her silence. Through Her smile, my soul went on a voyage in eternity. Slowly, joy and peace filled my heart and my cells vibrated in harmony with the universe. Even now, concentrating on the Mother, I can feel Her love as a flow of radiance.

Every daily experience has a meaning and develops our perception of the divine. Always in the background of my life I can live in Her energy which I feel as a real strength. I try to offer all experiences, whether good or bad. As we become more conscious, I think we understand that good or bad are the same: it is only our wrong-headed mind that sees a difference.

Thinking about Mr. Reddy, I recall his warm smile and intense devotion for the Mother. On many occasions we took a walk and like a child I would ask him the same question: "Tell me about the Mother – how did you meet Her?" His face would light up, he would begin to speak and then after a while he would become so flooded with Mother's love that his speech would become incomprehensible, so great was his devotion. In silence, his eyes would gleam. He was lost in Mother's love. All his words were for Her. His entire life was for Her. Never have I met a person so totally surrendered to the Mother. In many conflicts and difficulties I saw him stand unswervingly by Her; his inner faith never failed. Even if his mind and body suffered a great deal, his soul was in a state of offering to the Mother always.

Val D'or, Quebec

9.

An Angel Come From The Sky

It is not easy to speak about Mr. Reddy without speaking about the Mother at the same time. He was united to Her in every way.

I would like to have written a short chronicle of my friendship with him, with details and summaries of his "teachings" (for his conversations were, in a way, teachings). Unfortunately, I kept no record of our talks. But they have stayed with me and entered my soul.

There was something clairvoyant about his way of talking. Once when he was in the hospital in Bonn he saw that our activity on behalf of sick people was a good thing and would develop remarkably well. His speech would often be very wise as when he explained the Mother to people in ways suited to their stage of development and comprehension. At the same time he had the child's simplicity, the transparency of a pure bright and elevated soul. When pain diminished the endurance of his physique his silence was often more eloquent than any words for it was enriched by incessant and secret prayer; his smile was a sound you felt wrapped in. For all these reasons it was very sad to see the empty chair where he had been when we returned to Thalheim. Yet in the silence of his absence we realized he was still present, with his smile full of love. His death was only an illusion.

I remember when I first heard of him in December 1979–January 1980, and was told he was a "severe keeper". I was a little afraid that I might not be able to approach the Mother outside pranam and darshan. But my fears disappeared in front of Mr. Reddy's smile, so full of affection and understanding. At that time I was invited with three other Italians to a conversation with the Mother; Mr. Reddy was the last link of the translator's chain.

That scene is still very alive in my heart. I had received an unhoped-for gift, an exceptional reply to my timid prayer that God should number me among His children. To justify this last sentence I have to explain something. On certain previous occasions I had felt unjustly judged by a certain person; I felt profoundly hurt as I felt I had acted with the simplicity of a child and not at all with hidden purposes. I asked Mother secretly to help me understand if I was wrong or right.

I received a gift beyond my expectations; that day was Epiphany and there would not have usually been pranam and darshan. But Mother was going to receive some children and consented to us Italians attending the occasion and taking photos. Then there occurred, as I have related, the further gift of a conversation with Mother, Mr. Reddy and Adilakshmi.

It was a real day of grace. One other thing I remember with deep pleasure – a sentence told me by Mr. Reddy that remained in my heart as a flower blossoming, a sentence that emerged from his last deep silences. "Italian is as sweet a language as that originally spoken by the Mother." Then it seemed as if the ties that joined us to him and the Mother were eternal and could never be severed through all the shapes assumed by the soul in its becoming.

10.

Talk with Mr. Reddy

On one occasion when I came to Thalheim, I happened to meet Mr. Reddy. He was sitting in front of Mother Meera's house and was enjoying the nice summer evening.

I knew of Mr. Reddy from a previous conversation I had had with Mother Meera and Adilakshmi. Since the Darshan had not yet started, I took the opportunity to talk to Mr. Reddy. He looked at me with his brown brilliant eyes which radiated calmness and alertness, happiness and fulfilment. Even though he could not see properly, he immediately recognized me from my voice and my shape. I realized that he was a very sensitive man with a clear mind and a warm heart, and I felt immediate affection for him.

Talking for a while about Mother, I told him that I had a little present for Her. However, I was not sure whether She would like it and when I could give it to Her. He asked me to show it to him. He touched it and said, "The Mother will appreciate it," and gave me some advice on how to offer it to Her.

Taking Mr. Reddy's advice, I followed Mother after Darshan when She was leaving the Darshan room, although nobody usually does this. I said to myself that there are no limitations in Mother's life and that Mr. Reddy must know how Mother would react in this special situation. When I had reached Her, She turned Her head towards me and I handed Her the present. Never will I forget Her brilliant smile when I did so, realizing: Mr. Reddy knows Mother best.

11.

In 1977, I went to India for the first time, and I stayed there for two months. Without being aware of it, I lived in Mother's immediate vicinity; but I did not meet her. I was impressed, however, by the powerful, spiritual atmosphere.

A friend of mine, Frank from Essen, went to India together with other people. In a letter he wrote to me that "...the Mother is alive", which sounded rather peculiar to me. I thought he had had a vision or something of the sort. He came back after six months. We felt that there was a special radiation around him that was very impressive. So later, in 1979, four of us went to Pondicherry to see Mother.

One evening we passed by Her house on bicycles. We noticed a car coming from the other direction that was laden with flowers. We thought immediately that these could be no ordinary travellers. (It was Mother coming home from her first trip to Canada.) Mother, Adilakshmi and Mr. Reddy got out and said hello to Frank.

Three days later, we received our first darshan. There were about ten people. I knew immediately that Mother was an exceptional spiritual person. I felt a majestic, charming, loving, and very powerful presence flowing from her; my doubts were completely dispelled. Also, I had never seen such beautiful and shining eyes. Some of the people who had come had tears in their eyes.

After some time, Mother went away with Mr. Reddy who needed to get treatment for his foot. Three weeks later, Walter and myself also left for Kakinada. There we received darshan during five weeks which of course deepened our experiences very much. It was also the time of our first private contacts. Mr. Reddy's sense of humour and his attitude of devotion struck us. He spoke a lot about God and about yoga. He told us many little stories and parables.

On her second trip to Canada, Mother had a stop-over in Paris. We spent two hours with Her there, asking if we could visit Her in Montreal. She agreed. We had a wonderful time in Montreal. We also liked the city of Montreal as well as the whole country. Mr. Reddy remarked that Canada was the India of the West. Four weeks later, we asked Mother for the first time if She was inclined to come also to Germany. We were surprised when She simply answered "Yes".

I was in Montreal when Mother gave a "collective darshan" to about 150 people. She sat on a stage and filled the atmosphere with an extraordinary power. I was amazed when I realized the possibilities that are open to an avatar. Mother did not touch the devotees physically, and yet – I believe without doubt – She reached all the parts and levels of their being. We asked her about that particular kind of darshan, but we did not get an answer.

Back in Germany, we started preparing for Mother's visit. We rented a fairly large house on the outskirts of Essen where we all moved. Everyone continued their work or studies, respectively. Mother came in the summer of 1981. On the way from the airport, She said: "There is something..." Maybe She referred to something in the atmosphere. Also in Essen She gave darshan for four weeks. Some devotees came from Canada and Italy. On the last day in Essen She said: "I feel at home here." It was a great surprise for us.

We had rented the house for only one year. But there were also some difficulties with the owner, so Mother could not have remained with us anyway. She went back to Canada. One person from our group went along to arrange the trip. During that time we rented a house in a village in Westerwald, partly because we wanted to get away from the city. A lot of preparations were necessary to have the place ready in time.

Mother came in October 1981. We lived very simply. Heating was by coal and wood. Mother started to give darshan immediately every day, without any break. I did the shopping in a nearby town. There I felt as if I was from a different planet. Sometimes the shops in town made me tired; I felt such a contrast between home and the outside world. Later this got better.

It was in those months that Mr. Reddy fell sick due to his diabetes. Very often I took him to a doctor or to the hospital. Germany did a lot for Mr. Reddy's health, and I feel Mother appreciated that very highly. The summertime in Westerwald was very enjoyable. We had fruit trees, like plums, apples, cherries, and walnuts. The winter that followed was very severe (minus 20 degrees). There were only a few people at the darshans. On Mother's birthday there were about ten, which seemed like a big crowd to us. We also played table-tennis, but Mother did not like that so much. She said we fought too much.

At the beginning of 1983, Mother moved to Thalheim where a house was bought. I lived in a commune and visited Mother only off and on. There were doubts in my mind, but not in my heart. I felt immediately that this was my home. One day Mother phoned me and said I should come home.

From the end of 1984, we started different kinds of reconstruction in the house. One of Mother's devotees, an architect, had the necessary knowledge for that. The most wonderful thing was of course that Mother always worked with us. I felt as if we were little children playing in the sand. Mr. Reddy was sometimes there, too, sitting in a chair and watching us.

Mother Meera charmed us all with her presence. While working, we felt an inexplicable strength and joy. After the work we always had to clean up. One day Mother wiped the stairs on bended knees, and half an hour later She gave darshan. We asked Her once what were the rules in the house. She replied: "To be happy." She said that too many rules could enslave a person. Nevertheless, every one of Her devotees tried to be as disciplined as they could.

In my spare time I have always played a lot of music. More recently, I have also started to paint. I have an intuitive understanding of art. I feel Mother has been sending Her force to me through the walls, giving me joy and strength. It is like a rain, trickling down through the ceiling, tenderly and unobtrusively touching everything in its path. Adilakshmi says that we are enveloped by Mother's love, that we are basking in it without even noticing it. She also says that the love of Her children is the Mother's food.

To see Mother smile is one of the most beautiful gifts. Just a little smile of Hers gives us joy and strength for the rest of the day. Many visitors ask if we have seen Mother's smile, since they know Her smile only from photos. Sometimes we try to make Mother laugh. When we succeed we are happy.

A devotee who has been coming for many years says that with a photo one takes home some of the splendour and divine beauty. Many have also said that they felt the touch of Mother's hands on their heads even after several hours.

Before knowing Mother I had led a rather restless life. I moved often and changed jobs many times. To know her meant that I could organize my way of life better. I also started to understand that I didn't yet know much about life. But simultaneously She showed me the unknown possibilities of growth within and without. I decided to concentrate on the spiritual goal. Perhaps I had no other choice. She helped me to become a part of society. Again and again She helped me to get up when I had fallen. She gave me back my human dignity.

Mother's darshan means to face a mirror. It is direct, without sentimentality. It is an ever repeating "Day of judgement". Quite often I feel like a child holding on to Her saree. I also pray to Her inside in a simple way. Mother told us: "Always remember the Divine." One of my friends asked Her, how to do this. Mother said that it works best if you do it with your soul. My friend said that he couldn't do it just like that. Then Mother said: "Do it mentally or say it aloud." Once we asked Adilakshmi what we could do for Mother. She answered: "Be happy and love Mother, because love is nourishment for Mother." In 1988, I saw the start of big personal changes. They were the biggest changes in my life. No part of my being was excluded. Mother said: "If people will believe the experiences, then they must believe and trust you."

One time we asked Mother about physical and divine love. She said that there was only one love. One of my friends was a little rebel. Adilakshmi said, that this could also be a possible way to the Divine. But love, trust, and surrender are faster. One visitor from a different spiritual movement said, that next month "Celebration of the Divine Mother" would take place. Adilakshmi said with a glowing face that we had "Celebration of the Divine Mother" all around the year.

In India it is customary for friends to hold hands. Once Mr. Reddy did this with me. He asked me then: "Do you take or do you give?" I felt embarrassed and gave no answer. Mother jokingly asked me once what I wanted to become in my next life. I didn't want to know anything about this topic. Years ago I shaved off my moustaches. Showing it to Mother and Adilakshmi, they laughed without stopping. At the building site of the new house in Oberdorf I observed Mother with the workers. She told them to have a break. One answered: "Rest we will have when we are in the grave." Mother told him: "Neither will you have it then."

In our neighbourhood there lived a four-year-old girl. It was summertime and Mother's window on the second floor stood open. The girl shouted from below: "Auntie Meera, come down!" Immediately Mother went down, took her into Her arms and gave her chocolate. We were deeply moved envying her a bit. Then Adilakshmi said that when we would ask so innocently, Mother would come to everyone of us.

A forty-year-old friend of mine spoke with Mother about his relationships and emotional problems. At the end of the conversation he said that he felt like a twenty-year-old person. Mother laughed: "No, not twenty, but nineteen years old."

An elderly woman approached me after darshan. She had observed seven people coughing during darshan simultaneously. She wanted me to ask Mother if there was any special significance in this. We were amused but didn't pass the question on.

Once two visitors asked Her, if they could get realization in this life. Mother smilingly replied: "But you are only beginners." The spiritual ego was hit. Mother doesn't like it if people think too much about realization. She would like us rather to think about the Divine. Still we are pondering about it.

Once, four years ago, there were soccer championships. Mother said: "Yes, hopefully the TV's will all explode." Somebody came with a huge bunch of flowers and proudly said: "They are for You, Mother." Mother answered: "No, they aren't for me, they are for yourself." Another time I met a man in front of Mother's house. I asked him if he had come for darshan. He said: "If I enter this house, it might change my whole life!" He stayed outside. Mother, please give us the strength and patience to become your children.

12.

Mother Meera came into my life in spring 1982. But my search for Her started actually one year before, through a special experience. I had belonged to a large spiritual movement since I was 17, and had already lived in the centre for several years. It was on the seventh day of a silence that I was in the library and discovered a book the title of which electrified me completely: *Adoration of the Divine Mother*. I took the book into my room and read it in one sitting. It consisted of poems that were written in the presence of the famous South-Indian saint Ramana Maharshi. I didn't understand one word, I just continued reading. A completely new world seemed to open up.

Next morning when I woke up I had an argument with myself about the existence of Divine Intelligence in the world. As my arguments grew subtler, I suddenly felt the presence of the Divine penetrating my room; to my surprise it was clearly female! After some time I saw a golden spiral moving near the ceiling. Only years later I learned that the spiral was a symbol of the divine female principle. From then on I was looking for something I couldn't name or express, and it was connected with the Divine Mother. Not that I didn't have spiritual experiences before, I already had experiences of the Divine, I was used to the deep silence of meditation, but this seemed to be something beyond all of that. As my search grew stronger and stronger I wrote a poem. After I had met Mother, I again wrote a poem. If I compare these two poems, one is the answer to the other.

Meeting Mother

A friend took me to Mother. We had spoken about Her already, and I had heard about Her through another friend half a year earlier. Now he showed me a photograph. Mother's eyes jumped out of the frame at me. I slept fully charged with energy and on the next day a car was there, as if arranged, to take us there. At that time Mother lived near Koblenz in a small village called Kleinmaischeid (one year later She moved to Thalheim). The first time I just felt there was a lot of "power". The second time I saw Mother's beautiful smile, and after the third time

Thalheim, Germany 1994

I really felt wrapped up and floating in Divine Awareness. But I still wasn't convinced.

In the first year, each time I came just for "one more time". And each time I had some glimpse, some feeling, which was outside my normal experience. But then I had an experience which was quite simple. In meditation I saw Her standing on long stairs. It wasn't a vision, just a mental image. I stood a few steps behind Her. Now She turned, reaching out Her arms towards me. Her hand went right through my heart. From then on I knew, that I would always be, beyond doubt, infinitely connected with Her. In all the years when I was tested and many times tempted, very often with pressure, by the members of the centre to give up the contact with Her, it was this experience which made me persist in my relation to Her.

First years

In the beginning the activity was mainly in the heart. Before I met Mother, in my meditations I used to feel something in my heart but each time I came to a certain threshold, which I couldn't pass. After meeting Mother I could pass this threshold, feeling deep love which would penetrate my body. For the first time I felt I was put in contact with my soul, despite all the transcendences I had encountered before.

With Mother even the silence had an almost physical nature, much more tangible, while before it was more abstract, more mental. My spiritual horizon opened up. I started to have new ideas, new feelings, I could understand other people better, accept them more. I felt that all levels are spiritually equal, since the Divine is everywhere. So all people, meditators and non-meditators, spiritual or non-spiritual, were equal.

I actually felt that Mother put new feelings into me. As She says: "I also change human beings who have bad wills and bad characters." Thus Mother changes our inner programming, so that we can open up to the Divine in a new and more complete way. How marvellously my life has changed through this! Reading the instruction manual of a washing-machine is as interesting as reading a spiritual book. Everything can become a metaphor for the Divine.

Coming home

Ever since I came to know Mother, I had always thought about joining Her completely. But I was always afraid of living outside the spiritual atmosphere of the centre. After all, staying near Mother meant living and working in the outside world. To be near Mother was just not always possible, they were rare moments. The head of the centre was the first one to acknowledge Mother as the Divine Mother to a friend, even if not officially, in 1985. He had said: "Oh, so the Divine Mother is in Germany. It is very good to know Her to be there." In November 1985, I left the centre for the Mother.

Love versus emptiness

Once I had a dream which was very strange. In the dream there was a corridor and beyond that a vast field of emptiness. In this field there was a presence, a force, highly intelligent and refined. And it was clearly female. In order to come to that force, one had to traverse this field of emptiness. And the more one moved into that emptiness, the greater the pressure became. With each step the presence doubled. Even though that presence was highly attractive, I had to give up sometimes. After the dream for the first time in my life I had the impression that real progress was being made. This was the real work.

Not knowing what that force was, I preferred to call it the Divine Mother, since I want to see Mother everywhere anyway. Moving to Mother just meant this to me. Mother meant high energy, sweetness, while the world was full of emptiness. To go to Ma always meant leaving the secure atmosphere of the centre and going through mud. Even riding in a train and looking at houses and streets as they passed by created a strange aversion in me. Feelings came up which I had not known since I was a youth. Everything seemed so vain, the life of people so useless. And now the secure ground of the centre has been dragged away from under my feet! And at the same time there was this faint feeling deep in me, this faint vibration of Mother's love caressing me, as if to say: "Just have trust! I am with you."

It was a real adventure! There was this inner presence of Mother inviting me to follow Her and Her alone, and the outside world which was empty, and the aversion it created in me. And I was torn between these two worlds. I didn't believe Ma, when She said to me: "It is not the world that is wrong. It is your thinking that is wrong." There were so many uncertainties, fears: Would I be able to work eight hours a day? Would I find a job? Would I not lose all spirituality in this? And, would I really want it? I didn't have a profession, I had no money, no car, not even a driver's license. After all I used to meditate many hours a day.

The movement which had once helped me, had become a prison with golden bars.

Later on I recognized that this "emptiness" was just another illusion, created by a decade of fear to come out of the spiritual centre. Now any experience is quite possible riding in the Frankfurt subway, at work, while pop-music comes out of the radio, in a car. Experiences which were very rare even at the big group meditations, are now common in everyday life. Never again in my life will I fear the "outside" world, or a "bad atmosphere". And that is all due to the grace of Mother.

After about two months, I left the spiritual centre. I wasn't yet sure whether to stay with Ma. Then twice I was told by Ma that I could go back if I wanted. I figured a decision was needed. Still struggling within myself, I opened *Savitri*, that beautiful epic-poem of Sri Aurobindo, and came across this line: "I ask thee not to merge thy heart of flame/in the Immobile's wide uncaring bliss." That was the answer. I stayed.

With Ma at work

I was allowed to join the construction work, which was going on at Oberdorf. Mother was working there with a group of people every day for many hours. To work with Mother is something special. After work one may feel tired, maybe even exhausted, but full of joy and bliss. To be with Mother working at the building was nourishment for the soul. If you worked with Her directly, when finished for the day you felt high and drunk with Her presence.

Mother was working very hard, doing men's work. What is most astonishing is Her silence and focus during work. She would just point at tools, say one word, or make a gesture. The first time I came there, She showed me how to make big holes in the wall with a power-drill. Her radiance and light were always there, even during work. One time we, Mother and I, carried very heavy wooden plates from the ground floor up to the very top. It was a hot day, and there was a huge pile of them. I was very exhausted, and the more so, I thought, Mother must have been, since She is not really built like a man. So pausing after it, standing there with Ma, I suddenly felt an inrush of something like golden rain through my head. I was high from it for two days!

Mother also read our thoughts. Once I walked behind Her, thinking: "Why do You never look at me?" And She turned around smiling at me mischievously! Another time some of us were working for a whole day in one room and in the evening Mother came. I thought: "You don't even look at what we did." And She turned, looked into the room and came back! Still another time we were taking out cow-dung from an underground reservoir. While two of us were down filling buckets, Mother received them through a small opening in the floor. What an impression: Mother's face in the small hole receiving stinking and overflowing buckets. I always thought it was highly symbolic. Mother worked in the rain, unprotected, on a high roof without fear, on the scaffold. She joined in every possible kind of work, trying every tool or machine, showing that She didn't want to receive special treatment. Sometimes She would leave the work as late as 6:10 p.m., go to the other house, take a shower, get dressed and receive up to eighty people for darshan at 7 p.m., many of them new, coming for the first time.

Even if I could now see Mother every day at the building for almost a year, it was also a time of big emotional upheavals for me. I wasn't yet used to working, I was very unskilled, and very often Mother would send me to one corner of the building where I had to work by myself, while everybody else was working together with Mother. I had asked Mother to free me from jealousy, but I will never ask for that again. Nevertheless, at those moments, when I was alone, sad, quite often weeping, I felt Mother's presence most strongly caressing me. And very often then I found that She was just working next door unnoticed by me. In those moments of doubt and uncertainty – I had still been only a short time out of my old spiritual centre – I felt Mother's love and soothing care. Only my mind was looking for an outside proof, but inside in my heart everything was felt.

The moments when we were having tea with Ma after work are unforgettable. These sessions took place in half-finished rooms, everybody was sitting on bricks, or in summer outdoors by the little stream that flows through Mother's garden. If we were not speaking about construction problems, we were mostly sitting there silently, watching the birds in the sky and just enjoying Mother's presence. Then somebody would make a joke, and all would laugh, most of all Mother Herself. When everybody had finished the cake, Mother would get up and the party would dissolve.

Meetings with Mr. Reddy

The first time I saw Mr. Reddy was in 1982. I had a question regarding japa, and Adilakshmi went up to see Mother. After a while, she and Mother returned both supporting Mr. Reddy and sat down in the garden. We were invited to join and put questions to Mr. Reddy, which were translated by Adilakshmi. Mother just sat silently. Mr. Reddy told us about Mother, what is the difference between an avatar and a human guru, that She gives light to the whole of creation, not just human beings, but also the earth itself, the plants, the animals. Even the earth and the plants are more receptive than man. There is an ascending evolution of avatars. Each avatar would bring down a different level, like Rama, Krishna, Buddha, Sri Aurobindo and now Mother Meera.

Mr. Reddy seemed to know my thoughts and fears. So he said that japa (repetition of a divine name) protects you, helps you in difficulties and brings peace. (That was my main fear: I didn't want to live in the outside world.) He said that the simpler the form of meditation is, the better it is. And the more you learn about a spiritual system, the more you have to unlearn it. In the end you have to forget all about all techniques.

While we were talking, Mother sometimes looked at us silently, and Her glance went very deep into my heart. When Mr. Reddy stood up and Mother was supporting him, he said: "Look, how man is. He cannot even take one step without the Divine Mother." I clearly couldn't appreciate Mr. Reddy fully at that time, I thought he was just an old Indian man telling something.

The second meeting was half a year later in Frankfurt after a collective darshan on Mother's birthday. Mr. Reddy said that Mother was giving peace during darshan. I asked how the movements of darshan came about, and he said that they came about completely spontaneously, and that Mother was not imitating anybody. Again he had read my thoughts and answered my doubts. Mr. Reddy also said that some people would feel a lot and some nothing during darshan. But later they would feel Mother's presence in their lives. He also said that some people get many visions, but visions can be right and they can also be wrong.

A friend of mine said that he feels human gurus would be harder than Mother, maybe too hard. But Mr. Reddy said that also human gurus want only man's best and that they should be revered with gratitude. It was nice how everybody was sitting around Mr. Reddy, listening. It was a very family-like feeling and Mr. Reddy would tell a lot of secrets. I am not really the right one to speak about him, since I saw him only a few times.

The third time was in 1985. Three days a week an ambulance used to come and get Mr. Reddy at around 6 a.m. and he would come back at noon. One time when he came back I helped him out of the car with my friend. Obviously Mr. Reddy had become unconscious during the treatment. I was overwhelmed at the radiance which came from him at that time. It was just like being near Mother. I thought how a man who had just been unconscious, who was very ill, and who had to lie down, could radiate such an atmosphere. Mr. Reddy asked if Mother was present, and I jokingly wanted to say "no", when my friend pushed me saying, that I shouldn't make such jokes, since Mr. Reddy was serious about that question and he needed Mother more than anything else. Today I regret not having joined Mother earlier and in that way known Mr. Reddy better. He could have taught me so many things. When Mother was away, and I went to Mr. Reddy's samadhi, I got relief by feeling Her presence there. Sometimes I ask Mr. Reddy things through his picture and get an answer.

Grandiose reception

In May 1989, Mother made Her first visit to the United States. It is always special to go with Mother to the airport, She always seemed to be especially beautiful on those days. I was astonished when I saw Ma the first time in such a crowded place as Frankfurt Airport. I was walking behind Her full of bliss. On Her arrival back we had a little reception breakfast, and then the convoy of cars was going back on the German autobahn. There I found myself suddenly engulfed in a big ball of energy: Ma's darshan on the autobahn between two cars! It was a beautiful, sunny day, and when our convoy arrived at the street where Mother lived, colourful flags were greeting us from both sides, while flower-petals were covering the street. As we approached Ma's house, our cars had to slow down, because of a brass-band marching right in front of us. Germany spontaneously and unconsciously welcomed the Divine Mother back: it was a catholic procession going on. The new building itself was decorated by us with balloons showing words of gratitude and love. Mother seemed to be deeply touched, with moisture in Her eyes. Her love for Her devotees and children became obvious. We, of course, were very happy to have Her back.

At the end of 1989, the construction work came to an end. Not knowing what to do I went to northern Germany, to my sister's house. If I wanted to go back to Mother I needed a room, a job, and a driver's license which I didn't have yet.

After being away from Mother for a week, I felt powerless, not being sure what was going to happen. I read something about love, in a book of Krishnamurti. Suddenly Mother's presence was there, very powerful. That night I dreamt of Her inviting me to the house, standing in front of a certain room. I felt penetrated by the sweetest Divine Presence and love. Within two days I found a room near Thalheim, and within two weeks I had a job in a spiritual bookstore in Frankfurt along with another room there.

First I found Frankfurt horrible, but slowly, just accepting the change in the atmosphere, I learned to feel Mother's presence everywhere. I had many beautiful experiences in the city. Also I learned to deal with all the spiritual, and less spiritual, people coming to the shop, widening my acceptance of many spiritual paths. To open up to people was a great lesson I learned there. It was one more step into the world, which I had almost left behind me.

There I also had my first experience with Buddhism, while my spiritual orientation before was Hinduism or Vedantic. So, while reading a buddhist book after work in the shop, I suddenly felt a strong power coming down into my body, making me immobile. All questions that I had relating to buddhist philosophy were answered in an intuitive way. Somehow I made my way to my flat, when in the kitchen again I couldn't move. I was just standing there for an hour, observing myself, observing the power and my questions that were being answered inside.

At that time Mother had an operation. All people who came to darshan could visit Ma at the hospital. It was heartening to see Mother shaking people's hands as they passed by in a long row. I was astonished at the light and power She was emitting even in this situation. Even when She was ill, She nourished us, who were healthy.

Even if I could attend all darshans, commuting between Thalheim and Frankfurt, there was a pain, because I didn't anymore have that private access to Mother as before, when I was living in Her house. Mother had already moved to the new house, and at the end of 1990, a friend from my old movement wrote to me an invitation telling that it was possible for me to go back there. I didn't know if it would ever be possible to meet Mother privately again but I decided that I loved Mother more and stayed.

Mother had stated that She would not be a guru to anybody, but "if you need any help, like a mother I can help you, protect you". When my physical mother had died, She said She would always be my Mother. After some time I lost my room in Frankfurt, which meant I had to leave my job there. One week later, in the beginning of 1991, I had the opportunity to stay in Mother's house. I got exactly that room She had pointed out to me in the dream one year before.

With Mother's help I also got a driver's license. When I failed in the first test, my teacher said there would be ten testers. If I would get a certain tester I would pass, no matter what I did. I told Mother, and on the next test I got exactly that one tester and passed. I also got a new job in a printing company. This was the first real work situation, with normal workers, smoking, pop-music from the radio, and stinking paint. After the first week I thought I wouldn't survive. But soon it was apparent that Mother's light worked there, too, even in stronger ways than in the bookstore. And my fellow-workers, especially my boss, were very nice people, much friendlier than many of my "spiritual" friends. And at times the pop-music changed into some heavenlier tunes, and the smell of the paints into some divine perfume.

At celebrations people in Germany like to get drunk. It was unavoidable to attend such meetings in my company. Not drinking any alcohol myself, living on orange juice and mineral water that evening, I soon found myself in the midst of joking and laughing friends slowly opening up more and more to each other. I found that as one progresses spiritually one laughs more and more, and one of the most beautiful features of Mother is Her sense of humour. So, to the surprise of everyone I was laughing along, being drunk in my own way, drunk between two worlds, the spiritual and the mundane.

This was at the end of 1991. At this time I also had severe back-problems. For two weeks I couldn't work, and stayed mainly in bed. At this time I had an experience with Jesus. That was special because normally I have no affinity to him. I heard different chants, which had an influence on my subtle system, on different nerve-centres. At a chant of Jesus I had to weep, and felt deep love and also a deep pain in my

India 1979

heart. Telling this later to Mother, She said: "Yes, it had to be. He is God and you have to have love and devotion to him."

Now also more and more people started coming. One time, when a whole bus of people came unannounced from Belgium, a friend said jokingly to Ma: "Mother, now you will become famous." Mother answered: "I don't want to become famous!" In the beginning, when only a few people came for darshan, She had said: "Jesus had also only twelve disciples. But if one thousand people really long to see me, with love in their hearts, I will also take one thousand."

Ever since I came to know Mother, Her way of giving darshan has been the same. Regardless if there were seven or 170 people, She came down at 7 p.m., and took everybody's head in Her hands and looked into everybody's eyes until all had passed. In 1992, also Chandra Swami, a great enlightened sage, and his disciples came to see Mother. They did as everybody else in front of Mother, in all humility. We saw Ma being completely untouched by all the publicity created around Her. TV-teams would come to Thalheim, but Mother wouldn't give them permission to film or even an interview. Only very rarely have single journalists had an interview with Mother. During the last four years only two. But everybody could come to darshan. Rich or poor, famous or not famous, all got the same treatment.

It is touching to see Mother's spiritual action world-wide. She seems to be totally untouched by fame, just doing gardening or construction work in Thalheim. In 1993, Mother made two long trips abroad. At darshan time still a few of us would gather in the darshan room for a group meditation. I was so astonished at the light that came down on these occasions. Of course, we would miss Mother after some time, and I told Her afterwards, that I still feel very attracted to Her. She answered that if I wasn't attracted, I couldn't stay around Her. And whenever She comes back, I feel so overwhelmed especially at the first darshans. There are waves of warmth and love, light and power, flooding the room. And then again Her hands on your head, and those eyes, eyes you couldn't betray, which would always look into your innermost truth as if from eternity.

Mother will always be the sun of my heart. She has shown me real love and the beauty and the bliss of the Divine in a most tangible way. Apart from giving me Her own light, She has also shown me the light of my own soul. I feel more free now than ever before in my life. If I would

153

die now, I could say that I've had the most beautiful life. I am far from being perfect, but whatever difficulties remain, I know that they also can be removed by Mother's grace, if not today then tomorrow. In the meantime we can just enjoy and celebrate Her presence on earth.

13.

When back in summer 1986, I happened to hear about Mother Meera, I was in a sort of weird situation. Several years earlier I had quit my job in a governmental scientific research center in order to be able to concentrate on "a more spiritual way of living".

With this rather vague plan for my future I had lived in a meditation community for a few years. This was a very valuable time, an experience which I still estimate highly, but being a lone wolf basically, the restrictions and regulations of those surroundings were, after some time, felt to be too restricting. Thus I quit and thereafter had tried many things to find a compromise of earning a living without participating too much in this world.

When I met Mother the first time, I was without a job, felt to be in the wrong place on this unfriendly planet, and lacked any kind of good perspective. Also I was eager not to get into any claws of a "movement", or something like that, again!

Thus I came to Her house with a split brain: right-sided intellect cautioning, left-sided feelings looking eagerly forward to meet an "avatar". It was two minutes before 7 p.m., the time for darshan to begin, and the entrance door was already locked. I hesitated, but since I had rushed all the way at high speed, I could not accept to be defeated by a few seconds. Thus I rung the bell, and promptly I heard someone coming down the stairs. The door opened and with my usual voice I asked the young man who appeared, whether this was Mother Meera's house. He nodded and stepped back to let me in. Then he closed the door behind me, and whispered that darshan was from Friday to Monday, and one should come no earlier than 6:45 and no later than 6:55, and I should take off my shoes.

That was no surprise to me, because I was well acquainted with this Indian procedure, and the small entrance hall, filled with about a dozen pairs of foot-wear, from sandals to boots, was a familiar sight, strongly reminding me of my days around my Master. Well, I took off my shoes and began to explain why I was late, but he interrupted me and whispered, that we should hurry upstairs, because "Mother will come down any second!"

Thus, he took me upstairs, where I looked directly into a relatively small room, perhaps 4x4 m in size. Instead of a door there was a big opening to the hall. The whole floor, like the staircase, was covered with a white, soft carpet. Some people were sitting right on the carpet, some on round, thick cushions, but most people were sitting on folding chairs, which were arranged double-rowed along two of the walls in L-shape. On the third wall, surrounded by many flowers and covered with a white silk-cloth, a big, comfortable arm-chair constituted the obvious point of focus in this room. Over it, the joyful face of a rather young Indian girl smiled from a big photo; in front lay an oriental carpet strip, which I felt I should avoid stepping on, on my way to an empty chair in the corner.

The assembly had been sitting absolutely quiet, many with closed eyes. But when we came upstairs, a little stir of surprise went through the atmosphere, some shuffling and whispering started, some faces began to smile, some hands were raised in a subtle greeting... I don't remember exactly the number, but many of the assembled were very, very familiar to me from many hours of meditation and lectures together under different circumstances many years ago.

Before the stir was over and before I could sit down, a door was opened on the next floor and everybody hastened to get on their feet. A few moments later a tender young Indian lady in a beautiful white and red saree entered the room and without saying a word or looking around she went straight to the arm-chair and sat down. Another Indian lady of middle age, her secretary Adilakshmi as I learned later, had come in close behind the Mother, and she sat down on her own reserved chair, positioned behind the "waiting chair". Then everybody else took their places and all eyes, especially mine, were expectantly focused upon the young lady in the arm-chair.

She was sitting there, with an intense aura of silence and dignity around her. Her gaze was directed to the floor, she seemed to be completely collected within herself. This lasted for about half a minute, and I started to feel that gentle, but irresistable magnetic pull towards the silence of the Transcendence. I just wanted to give in and close my eyes, as in meditation and expected a long meditation-session, when suddenly Adilakshmi approached Mother and knelt down closely in front of Her bending forward and putting her hands on Mother's feet. Mother held her head with both hands, Her fingers on the temples, between Mother's knees. She closed her eyes and for something like a minute She remained like this, with a calm, but very concentrated expression on Her face. Then She loosened Her hands and Adilakshmi raised her head. She remained sitting on her heels, her face radiating, and now looked into Mother's eyes. This lasted for about another minute, then slowly Mother lowered Her gaze and for a few moments went into a state of rest. Adilakshmi bowed down to Mother and went back to her chair. She looked different, I would say sort of energized, happy, transformed...

Meanwhile, the person who had been on the "waiting chair", was kneeling on the carpet strip and was taken through the same procedure. After four, five persons it was clear that everybody was getting the same fully concentrated treatment of "prana" (=energizing) and "darshan" (=looking), some a little longer, others a little shorter.

As a newcomer I didn't want to interfere with any existing system of approaching Mother, thus I decided to go last. In the meantime I closed my eyes, enjoyed the very special atmosphere around Mother and had a very pleasant meditation. Then the waiting chair remained empty! With some nervousness I got up and moved forward. When I sat down only three steps from Mother, the idea that I was in the presence of an avatar suddenly made me feel quite small and pushed me into a substantial awe. My heart started pounding and my brain refused to function! But when it was my turn, I somehow managed to get down to Her feet and to hold my head in the right position!

All those inner turbulences didn't seem to disturb Her. I felt a firm grip on my head, which had the same effect as the firm grip of an expert coachman on the reins: the horses quickly came back under control! I felt calmness coming back and then joy bubbling up inside. Then the pressure of Mother's grip lessened subtly as if signalling: in a moment I will take my hands away! Though thus prepared I was somewhat sad, when She let go my head, too early for me.

With a little effort I forced myself to sit upright and open my eyes. I felt rather shy looking directly into Mother's eyes; it's quite an intimate exercise and I had never done this before with any person! In fact, in day-to-day life one doesn't find so many fascinating eyes, that one wants to read them, their stories often being too painful. Mother looked at me with big dark brown Indian eyes, and at my first glance the word "Infinity" shot through my head. These were not the eyes of a normal young lady: instead of a small pond I looked into an ocean. Now, I could try to explain this personal experience of mine with many words, and would most probably reap misunderstanding! Thus, I will only say: Mother's look has exactly that absolutely neutral quality, which doesn't hurt anybody, which allows one to remain open, which is soothing and healing.

At the end of my first darshan I bowed to Mother, impressed, happy, and thankful. I went back to my chair and Mother remained seated for one or two more minutes, without speaking or looking around, as if quietly blessing all of us. After Mother had gone up into Her private rooms, the assembly broke into happy giggling and laughing and joking. I said hello to my old friends, but soon left, because I needed to be alone with my overwhelming impressions.

From that day on I kept going very regularly to all darshans. But I knew Mother only "in office", not in Her day-to-day life. This changed, when Mother bought a huge building a few streets away from Her old house. Since the assembly was swelling rapidly, the old darshan facility was simply too small. Especially on Christmas or other holidays, people were piled up and down the staircase. It was quite uncomfortable and darshan lasted sometimes three, four hours. Even under these circumstances, Mother showed no sign of tiredness; the last got the same one-pointed attention as everybody else.

The "new" house was built around 1990, I guess, and had solid stone walls. It had been used before partly as a barn, partly as a cattle stable, but had now been standing empty for quite a while. Mother and a long-time devotee, who happened to be an architect, had made plans to build a three-storied house within the old walls, with quite a number of private rooms and, of course, a big darshan hall.

Since the financial budget was quite limited, Mother started recruiting volunteers, who had time and skill to help. Some years ago, I had collected some experiences in rebuilding old houses and I certainly had lots of time, because I still hadn't found a job. Thus I offered myself as a full-time worker to Mother. Some days later, after darshan, Adilakshmi told me that I was accepted. We also found accommodation in a neighbouring village, where a devotee had rented a small apartment. There I could stay during the week, while it was occupied on weekends.

I am not going to tell stone by stone how the house was built. We had lots of fun, but many weird or even painful things also happened to some people. All in all, I would say: It was quite adventurous! Many people had stepped forward, when Mother called, all motivated by the prospect of being close to Mother all day long. Many, I think, came with the true desire to recompense Mother for long years of Her support. Others were only curious. And perhaps half a dozen were not only of good will but also equipped with some experience and know-how.

Anyway, when the first workday came, the old barn was like a busy anthill. And Mother was there, not in a saree, but in pants and heavy shoes, wearing a smock and rubber gloves. An uninformed onlooker would have wondered about the young girl working hard and quite skilled in these surroundings. Nobody would have guessed Her to be the boss!

Speaking of Her perseverance and Her skill, I remember, how we built a brick wall, quite long and tall. This was on the third floor, maybe after ten or twelve weeks, when only a few workers were regularly available. The fastest way to set the bricks was: one person laying two strips of mortar, another person setting and adjusting the stones. I asked Mother to be my team-mate, warning Her that I was planning to go full speed. She giggled and said okay. Thus, I informed our handy-man that we would need lots of mortar, and off we went. The first two rows are for warm-up, I told Mother, please, put the mortar rather regularly and evenly thick.

Mother began and I watched Her and just made a few correcting remarks before I started setting the stones. After about half a row we got into a good routine, and from then on we just worked like little beavers. Almost no words were spoken, just complete concentration on the job. In the early evening we had almost finished our wall – and our handy-man!

Our working hours differed a bit from working hours on "normal" construction sites. In the morning we started rather late, usually around 10 a.m., but we didn't break for dinner until 3 p.m., and on darshan-days we continued until 6 p.m., on other days until 7 p.m. or even later. Then came the cake!

This was a most enjoyable rite, sponsored by the lady-devotees, who very regularly provided us with all sorts of cakes or cookies, or, if no such offer was in sight, then Adilakshmi baked a cake herself. Weather allowing, we sat behind the house on wooden logs or on the grass. Mother would cut the cake and distribute it on plates, while Adilakshmi was pouring out hot Indian tea. Mother Herself would only eat a small piece, and then look to it that everybody got the calories he needed! I must have looked pretty hungry every evening, or maybe it's because I am tall and rather skinny, anyway, Mother was always quite eager to hand me more. When all the cake was gone, She used to question me with a glance, and if She saw a need, pushed the crumbs in my direction! I felt I was being fed like a little bird and the procedure showed success: after nine months of it, I had gained about 5 to 6 kilos. Now I got a job and some years later, when I built my own house, after nine months I had lost 5 to 6 kilos! No cake-rites in the evening.

Speaking of food, I remember another situation, where Mother surprised us with a remarkable kind of humour, mark extra dry! We were putting the double panes into the windows. This special window was pretty big, and we had some problems to set the heavy pane correctly into the frame. Finally everything seemed to fit allright and the guy, who was in charge during this sensitive operation, began to set the holding wedges. All went well, but on the last stroke of hammer, the pane broke! Now, this was a really big double pane, which had cost quite a lot of money. We stood frozen in silence, when Mother suddenly produced a short, sort of diabolic giggle and, pointing at the poor fellow, remarked cooly: "No food tomorrow!" That broke the silence!

In a way, Mother in Her private life seems to be like "in office": She is rather taciturn. There is a dense aura of silence around Her, and Her reactions to happenings in the surrounding usually are quiet, if at all perceivable. But I remember two occasions, where I managed to elicit some stronger reactions from Her.

Here was Mother working on top of a ladder, which was, as we felt, blocking our passage through a door. We squeezed through the small opening, but finally we had to carry a long board through the door. So I informed Mother that we needed to move the ladder, not much, just out of the door. When She started to climb down, I said: "No, no, just hold on to the ladder, I'll quickly lift you both over." The quy beside me gasped in terror, I don't know whether he saw Mother falling or whether he was shocked by my disrespectful offer. Anyway, before he

159

could stop me, I lifted Mother and the ladder a few inches up, made two steps aside and let Her down again, jolt-free, as I'd hoped. Mother obviously had enjoyed the trip, She was giggling joyfully.

Then there was this awfully hot summer day, when we all took a pause in the shade behind the house. I was setting a wall of big heavy bricks that day, and in order to avoid scratches I was wearing a shirt with long sleeves. I was quite steaming and very much in need of a quick cooling. Actually, a cold shower would be very nice! Inside the next room lay a water hose. I went in and pulled my shirt off. Then I realized there were sacks of cement, which ought to remain dry. Thus I threw the water hose through the window opening, opened the water faucet and quickly ran out to take the refreshing shower. People were not quite sure, how to react, but when Mother exploded into laughter, they followed quite relieved. Nobody else wanted to take a shower, though.

There are many more incidents coming up in my memory. It was such a happy time to be around this enlightened soul. Like myself, probably all, who had that privilege, will call it the most valuable time in their lives. It takes about nine months for a new human being to come to life, after my nine months with Mother I also felt like newly born. Thank You, Ma!

14.

A wise man once said: "Does my speech nourish me or does it weaken me?" Now, what is there to say without "weakening" oneself? Mother teaches in silence. Teaches? There are no lessons, there is Darshan. What is Darshan? Can one dare to really describe it – hardly! From the outer view one could perhaps describe it as a bodyless birth in no time. What happens when... When you sit on your not too comfortable chair or on your cushion on the floor and try to meditate – which is quite different each time. It seems you make the vague decision to get up only in order to sit down on the floor again afterwards. You forget the reason, the goal, the hard cold floor. You become only your heart-beat There is no doing. IT is doing. IT is leading you to the waiting chair, where you most humbly wait for your turn. Then after kneeling down – in the midst of all light – before the Mother of all Mothers, there is sudden darkness. Back in the womb? Your head and forehead feel fingers penetrating streams of love and compassion through your inmost being, stopping thoughts, wills, intentions, requests, prayers. IT

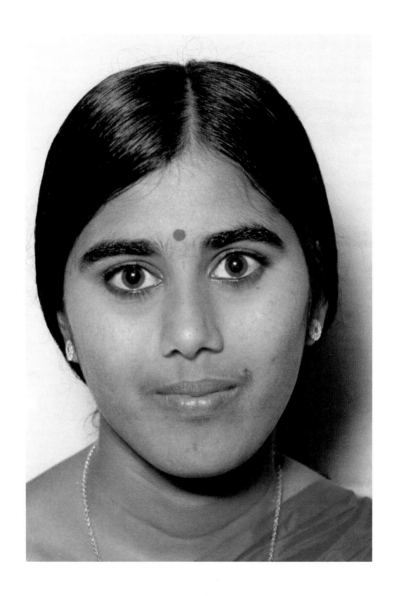

India 1979

raises your head, and you try to look – your outer eyes meet eyes allright. But are these eyes? You seem to recognize your own Self which is leading you to its origin. How long does it last? Seconds or eternities? There is some pain when these eyes – full of love and blessings – lower their lids and you leave this place of divine shelter incarnated by the Mother.

You stagger back to your seat over legs, arms, bodies, and scattered wardrobe. Are you still the same? Of course! Same arms, same feet, face, body... inside however – your insight has been turned upside down. A glimpse into the Universe has taken place – that is Darshan.

They are perhaps "weakening" these lines, no doubt, but Adilakshmi asked me to write down something for her book – "you are staying at home, so you can write." This is, in all humility, what I am able to say.

15.

Dearest Ma,

With gratitude and happiness I am seeing that all the beauty, tenderness and affection are the outcome of Your Being, that all I do, perceive, and experience is an act of Your grace.

The miracle began an evening in autumn 1984. In a small room of Your house in Thalheim, Langgasse, I was waiting for You. Exactly at 7:00 p.m. You came to make us happy with Your darshan. I fell in love without any resistance, deeper and deeper. You were full of beauty, freshness and indescribable sweetness. Don't ask me what is the meaning of darshan. I don't know. The happenings are so immense in these moments while one is genuflecting and the tenderness is flowing from Your soft fingers which soothingly hold the head and when Your divine eyes are drying all tears of life.

This first evening I was running like a child who had missed his mother for a long time. The inconceivable was happening: golden-red rays of fire were flowing from Your divine eyes which shook my body and all my consciousness was spiralling overhead. I was shocked but in a most beautiful way. Tears didn't come to an end.

The next evening I came full of expectation waiting for repetition or for the next great surprise... in vain. Without any hesitation I went to one of Mother's devotees in order to complain of not being satisfied. So I have learned that those experiences are divine gifts. They have nothing to do with effort, punishment, or reward. After that I had the chance to visit each darshan and most often what I experienced was being plunged in white or golden light. At night I would wake up, flames erupting out of a volcanic sea and taking their course along the spine, and around me there was nothing but innumerable dancing golden dots.

I became careless, forgetting Your splendidness. My vanity was increasing, ending in thoughts like "Soon I shall have reached the spiritual goal". But Your doing – not my noisy work – was going on in silence. I perceived the other side of the coin: hatred, jealousy, vanity, envy. The light showed me what was existing in the darkness of my consciousness. There was no escape from them. Light and darkness changed and the goal was moving into a far distance.

Together with a girl friend we had the grace to see Mother again and again. For a long period each homeward journey was accompanied by a mood of ecstatic drunkenness.

At Christmas I had the desire to get a present for You. While shopping I met You, Adilakshmi and a young Indian man – Adilakshmi's brother – in Frankfurt. Without talking to each other, a single glance and I was plunged in, let me call it, *ananda*.

On Christmas Eve after darshan You made me happy by allowing me to visit You in Your apartment. Only You and I. I couldn't speak enough English to express myself in words, so I could just look at You.

There was only looking. My nerves were vibrating because of the excitement. I felt an immense power and became anxious that my whole being would explode and I felt the desire to run away.

One day You made me happier than other times by allowing me to stay overnight in Your house. From then on I lived with the desire to be near You. This unspoken desire was fulfilled and soon I was allowed to come every weekend and remain there.

Often Your guests were in high spirits like children. Once we were shopping and after that we visited a café. We were sitting on the terrace. The air was trembling. I repeated Your name "Meera, Meera, Meera". Without any distortion the eyes were attracted by the sky and in its vast blueness there appeared in gigantic size a spot like a peacock eye in blue-golden and green colours. Often I was accompanied by sprinkling dots and dashes in thousands and thousands, sometimes silver and sometimes golden.

For all that the shadows in my consciousness did not cease. And from the heights I was falling to the depths. I refused to work with those shadows and I became angry with You. Sometimes I left You – outwardly – but nevertheless I had to return because of Your love.

During darshan often You became greater and greater and the distance seemed to increase. At those moments Your radiant beauty was not of this world. I cannot but cry being touched by this indescribable gentleness and warmth.

When I had to visit others and I informed You about my doings I got Your blessings and the meetings took an astonishingly harmonious course.

I admire Your immense skill in all things that You are doing, Your overwhelming simplicity, Your gracefulness, Your endless vastness, Your silence, and Your never-ending love.

Thoughts, emotions, moods – they are changing all the time but at this moment I love You with all my heart. My life with You is sun, wind, and storm. I hope it will never come to an end.

16.

Before my wife and I met Mother Meera, we went to meditation courses where we felt always at home. On the last course in Holland something changed. We were talking about not feeling comfortable, we were like foreigners on this course. One day before the end of the course two participants next to us were saying that there is a saint in Germany whose name is Mother Meera. When we heard this, immediately we tried to find out the address and to hear what this saint would do. But nobody could explain what really happens in darshan.

We had the idea of driving directly from Holland to Germany to get darshan. It took quite a long time to find the place where Mother lived but we arrived in time. We were sitting in the midst of about twenty devotees and waited to see what would happen. We felt in this house a warm, silent and energetic atmosphere.

I remember my first darshan at this evening. I was nervous and felt that I came to rest, when Mother held my head in Her hands. When She looked into my eyes, my first feeling was: "This is it, what I have missed without knowing all these years." It was a feeling of being at home. For me it was amazing, that I had not been aware of this during all these years.

That night we drove home and decided to come more often for darshan. The impression from that night lasted for some days. I felt happier and more lively during my daily activities.

From time to time we went for darshan and the results built up. I felt that another quality came up, which I didn't know from meditation. Before, the main emphasis was on the time spent in meditation. Now it was also during the daily activities, that I felt more happiness and energy.

We were lucky in that Mother Meera had not yet lived very long in Germany, and so Her house was not finished. It is my business to construct buildings and so it was natural that I would help during the weekends to work on the house.

I was very happy to have the opportunity to work with Mother. Quite often She was present and also working. Mother had Her own way of working. She was working silently, but with concentration and precision. I tried to learn from this, also to work in this way and I think that with time I became more peaceful and more silent in activity also during the week at home.

One of the most important changes for me during this time was that I began to accept my life as it is and it became dearer to me. Before I met Mother I used to reject activity because it disturbed my silence. Gradually during the years it changed and I began to like the day which began every morning.

Through the darshans and the time spent with Mother I learned much about myself. When I was with Mother I often saw clearly my good and bad sides. I saw my own reactions with their motivations. When it was hard to see my own mistakes, always Mother seemed to know this and some warm energy came up and it became easy.

Mother is for me a living example that one can live a normal life with all one's duties and maintain silence, love and happiness.

I never met anyone, who could better listen than Mother, when I had problems. Mother hears what one has to say in an open, silent, and neutral way and the answer is very short but exact. So often I saw how much love Mother gave to everyone who came to Her. No matter what the circumstances are, Mother gives everyone what he or she may need with love.

It was a great impression for me to see that Mother's love is love, that doesn't expect anything in return. Never did I feel, that this love was dependent on some outer thing. It is not a love which is like glue, Her love doesn't bind.

To feel with others is one quality which is obvious in Mother. In my own life I felt that this ability came forth a little bit. At home, the energy and happiness that came forth more and more gave me the possibility to be more friendly with my environment and to see a little bit more what it needs.

I am most thankful, that in my life there is an increase in the kind of happiness, which is not dependent on any circumstances, which comes from inside without outer reasons.

Sometimes friends ask me to speak to Mother about their problems to get help. In most cases they feel relief immediately at the time when I ask Mother. Even in cases, where the persons don't know, that I ask for them, they tell me, that their problems have been solved or they feel relieved.

Mother doesn't speak much, She is very silent. But when She speaks, it is at the right moment and with words that illumine me. In these moments I have the feeling that I realize something and see it and understand it in a very simple and clear way.

Quite often I ask Mother for help and my problems get lighter and resolve often totally. I believe that Mother knows exactly, when a soul is in a bad condition. An example of this is when Mother was in America. My mother was very ill in a hospital and I got very depressed. When I came home from a visit to the hospital I heard on my telephone answering machine Mother's voice: "How are you?" That was all. But when I heard these words my suffering was gone immediately and the inner tension relieved so that I started crying.

When She came back from America I asked Her what was the reason for Her phone call. She said: "I felt that you were in a bad condition."

Often I think of Mother and ask inwardly Her help. Mostly I feel energy, warmth, and lightness which come with satisfaction. The situations are then no longer so pressing and their importance vanishes. Other devotees have also had the same experience with the same results. I think that anyone who inwardly turns to Mother with sincerity gets help on every level.

Some time ago I told Mother that I have some fears of illness, of loss... She only said, seriously: "Fears are not good." After some time I became aware, that my fears were almost all gone. It was such a relief, that I could with joy enter situations which had caused fears before.

Along the years my vision has changed. I have begun to live more in the present. The past is further away. Also the future is no more so interesting. Now I feel more freedom in the present.

17.

In the beginning of January 1986, I learned about Mother Meera. I was 35 years old and my life had quite a lot of painful experiences. At the first darshan I saw that everybody was allowed to come to Her, the Divine Mother. Nobody had to fight to get darshan, it was just easy. When my turn came I was very impressed. I felt the power of the divine love and my inner blocks were falling away. I understood my past. I saw my past life as an old movie. Now it had become lighter and I didn't have to suffer with the movie actor. In the following months more of the feeling stabilized, that I was finally at home. I began to feel very good, safe like a child in the house of her mother.

My daily working hours at this time were long, up to 60 hours a week, but I could go for darshan or I could think about Mother and get relief.

In many crises when I didn't find a way out, I asked for Mother's help. Immediately when Mother knew the problem, a deep power pushed away the things that caused the problem and everything began to come in order without any personal effort of my own.

By that time some of my sorrows in life, like my three children, changed from sorrow to pleasure. My daily life became easy and enjoyable. The laugh of the Divine Mother has a magnetic attraction for me. Every darshan is an elevation to the divine worlds without pain or suffering, like heaven on earth. I wish for my life the support of the Divine Mother and I know that every request of mine is responded to by Mother with a smile.

18.

During the first darshans I didn't feel contact with Mother right away, but since I have started to entrust myself to Her I am sometimes able to experience Her love and strength.

This love heals, it heals old wounds of my childhood. There is no more a place for complaints and a gratitude arises. This gratitude and Mother's love have begun to change my behaviour and attitude. I really feel ashamed of my complaints and try to develop an attitude of love and help. It works. I enjoy a new relationship to my family and my worries and troubles disappear more and more. It is a feeling of freedom.

The experience of Mother's love gives me the wish not to act for my own satisfaction. This wish gets often out of sight, but there is a change in the way I act. I feel protected and the confidence in Her is a great source of help and love.

Since one year I take more often part in Darshan. During the Darshan I have a big wish to experience Mother's love and power directly. But I have many thoughts, good and bad, in my mind or I try to understand Mother's look. So busy with myself I often experience only little.

Sometimes, in unexpected moments, I feel the presence of Her deep love. This love goes through my whole being, it makes me shine. This experience of love has healed my old wounds; I look back on this process with astonishment and gratitude. And fortunately we've also found a new way of being together in our family.

I prayed for Mother's help, force and guidance during a very difficult and strenuous examination. Afterwards I felt these exam days were two of the happiest days I have ever had. To experience Mother's support is simply wonderful. It is a great gift for me to pray to Mother, to ask for Her love, help, power, and support. I feel myself protected and at home wherever I am. From the depth of my heart I thank Her.

19.

Dear Adilakshmi,

Here are some words concerning Amma and Her help in everyday life. You ask us to be brief? You may as well ask us to put a huge oak tree back into the acorn out of which it came! Her help is by the minute now!

We needed somewhere to live, which was quiet and suitable for not possessing a car. Mother found it for us. In a quiet town in a peaceful valley in the countryside. It was not even advertised, we were led to it. It is perfect.

Being away from my country of birth for many years I thought I was not eligible for social benefit at a certain age. Mother, one day, turned me into a government office building to make, I thought, a hopeless enquiry. Six months later all was somehow completed and I received what I had thought was impossible.

My daughter was expecting her first child. She was not a young woman and I had been told there would be need of extra medical attention. I wrote to Mother for help. I was in India for the birth and was the only person allowed to be with her, so I witnessed the help of the Divine first-hand. A smooth birth in very special surroundings, with no complications! To top it all, the gift of a beautiful baby girl. My deepest gratitude, Mother Meera, for all that comes from You.

For a few months I had been wanting to give Mother some jewellery which I had quite believed for many years, was a security for me for the future. I was slowly coming to realize that the Divine is our only security. On my birthday, a beautiful warm day, the first for weeks (a gift from the Mother?) I asked for this jewellery, diamonds, to be offered to Mother. A feeling of great peace and joy flowed through and around me. A short time after, I was sitting on a bench not far from Her home when Adilakshmi approached smiling very broadly and began speaking to me and thanking me for the gift to Mother. Such a warm conversation. Imagine my astonishment when next evening I arrived for darshan, Adilakshmi quietly put something into my hand and said: "The Mother says you should have these and She has blessed them." It was the diamonds! I found it a beautiful example of Divine Reciprocation – take one step towards the Divine and She will take ten towards you.

Dear Adilakshmi, how can I stop these tears? I can't write for them! Oh, aren't we blessed!

20.

On the first occasion that we visited Mother to receive darshan we had only been given very approximate directions on how to reach Thalheim. We had been given a slip of paper on which was written DORNBURG/THALHEIM. We had travelled by train as far as Koblenz, then towards Limburg, but by about 5 p.m. we had only reached Diez, where we knew there was a youth hostel. We decided to stay there and enquire next day. Our train broke down in Nassau and, as we spoke virtually no German, we were aided by a young, English-speaking Lebanese refugee who lived in Diez. He also took us to the youth hostel which turned out to be an 11th century castle, beautifully restored. Next day we were looking for Dornburg/Thalheim at the tourist information and were directed by bus to Thalheim, via Limburg. We had Mother's telephone number from the book *The Mother* by Adilakshmi and phoned to ask what we should do now. It was then we found we were calling from opposite Mother's house and one of the devotees kindly took us into some accomodation in Dorndorf. Only later did we realize that each and every step, each and every person, had been moved by Mother's will. And since then, over and over again, the pattern has been repeated. Often my faith is lacking, so often I become fearful and doubt – but *always*, without exception – Mother is there and the result is there. And this has become the pattern of our life, in everything. Our work, our standard of living, our entertainment, every minute detail of our life has in it, at its base and as its driving force, the power and the hand of Mother.

In September 1988, I underwent major heart surgery in England and during the days of recovery immediately I saw quite clearly Paramahansa Yogananda looking down at me and speaking with an old man with a long white beard. It was nearly two years later that I first saw a photograph of Sri Aurobindo and recognized him as the old man in my "dream". It was in December 1988 that we were first called to darshan by Mother Meera. At this darshan we realized that our guru Paramahansa Yogananda had sent us to Mother. My health since then has been excellent and all medical tests etc. confirm that I am now 100 per cent fit.

Travelling to darshan meant for us a journey of 12 hours – four trains and a bus ride. Something made me look at the timetable again and I saw (Mother clearly showed me) how we could shorten the journey by over two hours going and coming. It was also much cheaper.

In my work as a Pharmacist, some wrong tablets were given out. I had no way of contacting the patient (no name, etc.). I prayed to Mother for help, because it would have been very dangerous. Within five minutes the patient came back into the pharmacy and said she had dropped the bottle of tablets and broken the lid – could I please replace it. We were able to replace the tablets, too, and avoid a serious situation.

Many times in my work I find "things happen" as if in a kind of "swirl" around me and serious dangers, of which I was totally unaware, are mysteriously avoided. I know it is Mother who does this and I am now familiar with this "feeling" that comes.

I had applied for work, which I had been told was available. The man I spoke to said it was no longer there, but I had already committed a lot of money for travel etc. to the job. I rang Adilakshmi and asked her to ask Mother for help – would Mother hold my hand (for I *am* Her child) when I rang again. I phoned, the man said he could be of no help – then to my utter astonishment (and his!) he created a job for me and made the necessary arrangements so I need not lose my investment.

Returning from darshan, in a very tight travel schedule, we were waiting at Koblenz for our train, due on platform 5 at 9:53 a.m.. At 9:52 my wife and I both felt our heads turned, as if by a mysterious force, to platform 4 where we saw our train, ready to depart. The conductor held it for us as we boarded. Unannounced, the train platform had been altered at the last minute for technical reasons.

Always we hear Mother speak to us in our hearts. It is not a voice, not a "communication" that can be described in human terms. It is a certainty, a directive – sometimes only clear *after* the event. But always it is there. We are aware that what Mother said in *Answers* is an actual fact: "...and at every moment be prepared for miracles".

Thalheim, Germany 1994

21.

This is an extract of my experiences and my journey with Amma Meera. These are my own individual experiences. They can be quite different for other individuals. Everybody is called to make his own experiences.

Since childhood I was afflicted with a question: "Why? Why do I live? What is the meaning of life?" I saw the difficulties of my parents and relatives. I saw my own problems and had of course my own ideal imaginations. No one could answer these questions of mine. What should one do as an adolescent person? One becomes either a rebel or yields to drugs or searches for the truth in one of these new theosophical societies. I tried simultaneously two or three of these societies because it was actually clear to me from the beginning that my life must have a destiny that has something to do with God. The modern idea that one takes birth, then a little later dies and that is the end of life was something absolutely impossible for my mind to understand. Even the new religions have the same terrible defects as the old ones. They are *dogmatic* and some of them are even worse.

As I noticed that all my strength and enthusiasm were getting exhausted, the whole world collapsed for me. At this moment, Amma came into my life. Some old friends showed me Her photo and invited me to visit Her for a darshan along with them. Her photo had attracted me very much and I visited Her. From then onwards darshan was like an addiction for me. At the beginning it had a very positive effect on me. Every time after the darshan, I was filled to the brim with happiness and energy. This way, Amma helped me to come away from the new religions.

Mother does not speak on a way of life nor does She dictate any dogmatic rules. In my situation this was very important for me. This has led to another important phenomena, i.e. I started hearing more and more my inner voice.

Slowly I lost the urge to go for the darshan. Partly because of convenience, and also because the flow of devotees started increasing. But I felt a strong closeness with Amma which I could further strengthen through japa. So my life was an interplay between existing in closeness with the Absolute (God, Paramatman, Source of life) and my old behaviour pattern. This interplay is still existing, leading me through intense ups and downs in my existence. In other words, I am more intensely confronted with the difficulties and problems of my existence.

On the other hand, limitless confidence in Paramatman is growing, giving more and more peace and a fearless life. Hopefully, this expands further and so fills my whole existence.

Latent in these lines are not only several experiences, but also the books that I read, and of course the time. For me, knowledge from books is true only when it works. But to try out is fun!

Mother told me once, that I should be patient. It was very difficult for me to realize this. But life is the best school.

Do not forget to love! To be in unity is nothing but LOVE without limits.

22.

Mother Meera and some devotees accompanied Adilakshmi, who went to India. At the airport a trolley with rather heavy luggage had to be moved from the underground to the first floor. On the escalator, at the moment when I had to hold my trolley with all my strength, immediately Mother was there and helped me to balance it and everything went on perfectly and easily.

Always in difficult or dangerous circumstances, at once Mother Meera is there. When devotees helped building the house in Oberdorf, Mother did the dangerous work. She helps always in difficult situations.

Before the first meeting with Mother Meera, I sometimes had a hard attitude and judgement towards younger people and everyone around me who was normal. In a lovely way, She let me see what was wrong in acting like that. I learned from Her little by little how to act with love and patience, even with myself. Thanks to the Mother and Her help, my behaviour has changed and is still changing more consciously. Mother makes me free and teaches me to respect the freedom of others.

For several years, I had inner difficulties with a relationship I had with a married man. I knew from the beginning that he was married and I was convinced that he would never leave his family and his business. Although we loved each other, I was not sure if this was right. I was tortured for a long time and I wanted to speak with Mother about it.

Then all at once, She was there and nobody else was in the room, but I dared not. Some days later, I again had the same opportunity. I asked Her if I could continue this relationship and She told me that it was not good, that the man formed a unit with his family. At that moment I felt sorrow but most of all an indescribable freedom and Her immeasurable love. During the following days, although they were hard, She gave me what I needed to get over it all. Mother Meera teaches me to trust Her, to love the Divine. She gives us all that we need at the right moment and She is always there when we need Her.

I thank Mother Meera that She is with us all on this earth. I wish that I could learn to love Her, the Divine Mother, in the way She wants.

Many thanks to Adilakshmi, who is always so helpful.

23.

When I left the army (for me a time full of humiliation and scorn) the difference of being with Mother was amazing. It was the first time I had worked with Mother. What I remember most was Her inconspicuousness, Her simplicity, Her knowing everything on every level. These were the first happy days in my life.

During the construction of the house a bar had to be knocked into the ground with a huge hammer. Nobody would hold the bar because I was knocking and they didn't know me yet. There were about eight persons there and when I asked for help, somebody said that he didn't dare to help. At that moment Mother said that She had a lot of faith in me and She was holding the bar while I was knocking. This strengthened my self-confidence in a great way and I still think of this now a few years later.

In finishing the roof we had to put plates on the chimney. I took six plates and after searching, put these plates on in a nice way. I asked Mother to come and see. She took everything away. I was unhappy and said nothing. While I was looking at Mother, there came an inward tranquillity in me asking me just to look, it was after all Mother's house. When Mother was finished, She had needed five plates and they were put in a better way than before. After that Mother looked at me as if we had made this together. As the work advanced I became better and better in the work as well as in my inner being.

When I went home after being with Mother Meera for a month, I was listening to the radio. Eveyone and everything was fixed on an unimportant football competition and involved in it. On that moment, with the memories of Mother Meera fresh in my mind, I knew how many times we (as human beings) give much value to stupid things.

Now that I have been with Mother Meera for a long time, I feel that there is something constantly working in me. Sometimes I feel depressed and when I call on Mother, it disappears as snow in the sun. And every time I go home from darshan I feel enormous love.

24.

Since I met Mother Meera, I find it a little easier to understand what the Divine is. Before, the Divine was more abstract. With Mother the Divine gets a more personal, more concrete dimension.

I remember a day when Mother, Adilakshmi and Herbert came back from a journey to India. Several people, who live with Her in the house in Thalheim, came to the airport to welcome Her. Mother and Adilakshmi arrived first. We were waiting for Herbert. When She stood there with us in silence, I felt such a strong power and joy. I had never felt anything like that before. I thought we were giving Her flowers and wanted to be there to welcome Her but in fact She was giving. I also remember with pleasure the days when we were working in Her house in Oberdorf. We were not obliged to work. No, we were free to do what we wanted. Mother worked with us, always in concentration. She was doing all kinds of work: from cleaning and sweeping the floor to cutting tiles. Sometimes in summer She came and sat in the garden. Often several people from Her house came to sit with Her. She was listening to us, laughing, and sometimes telling jokes.

When I am in the house in Oberdorf and I have questions about something in my life and want to ask Mother about them, I have experienced several times that She passes my way. For example, I see Her walking in the garden or working in the house, so I have the opportunity to ask Her. She really wants to listen and help if you ask Her something. I hope I am conscious enough to know how lucky I am to know Her and to have the chance to stay with Her in Her house.

25.

Dear Mother,

When I came for the very first time to Your darshan my heart was throbbing with excitement. After a while, suddenly there was a complete silence inwardly and outwardly, totally unexpected, fresh and new. Later, on my way home, other people who were at Mother's darshan questioned me: "How do you feel after the first darshan?"

I told them about the marvellous perpetuating silence, that was there, gentle but at the same time powerful. They looked at me perplexed and wanted to know the meaning of it. Now I understood: Dear Mother, You have given me a divine present.

At the same time, You have given me again and again everlasting joy in life and a confirmation burning inwardly, that the good will realize itself here and now.

With an inexpressible gratitude I feel obliged to You, dear Mother, also for the marvellous eternal love which is enveloping us all.

26.

It was summer 1991 in Stockholm, Sweden. I was preparing to leave for a holiday. I was to visit a Russian Ortodox monastery in eastern Finland. I often used to stay there during summer for a few days enjoying the scenic beauty and the eastern hymns and reliving my old fantasies about meditating in Himalayan caves. I called a good friend of mine on the phone. He told me that he and another friend of mine had been to Germany and seen a wonderful holy person, a woman, who had made a deep impression on them. I naturally got interested right away. My friend had a book with him called *The Mother* by Adilakshmi and after some persuasion I succeeded in borrowing it to take with me.

Finally after a twelve-hour ferry trip to Finland and the following eight-hour drive I was in my room in the monastery. "Great," I thought, "this is what I call living." I made myself ready. I lit some incense, took a comfortable position, checked that chocolate and soda were within easy reach, and started reading the book. And it was like stepping into another world. Sometimes I laughed out of joy, sometimes tears were rolling down my cheeks. I had read most of the spiritual books there is to be read during my years of meditation but this was different. This was so concrete and real. And it was about a person who was in the body, living relatively close to me. During the last few years of my spiritual life I had had the feeling that some change was going to happen, something new. The problem was that I didn't have the faintest idea what and when. Now here was something. I decided that I, too, would go and see Her.

* * *

A week before my first trip to Mother I had the following experience while sleeping: I found myself in a room full of people, all waiting for Mother's darshan. There was a long line but at last it was my turn. I kneeled before Her and She put Her hands on my head. I felt Her merging into me, She was as if inside me and started talking to me. I said I had come with a friend of mine and was there for the first time. She asked about me, what was my name, what kind of work I did etc. She smiled and nodded approvingly to my answers as if indicating that everything was all right. Then She looked into my eyes for a long time. The intimacy that I felt with Her at that moment is hard to describe. It was as if I had known Her for a long, long time, as if I had found a long lost close friend.

Then we went into another room. We were alone in the room, sitting on the floor and talking when a short, stout man entered. I had no idea who he was. (Later, after having come to Mother a few times I suddenly realized that it must have been Mr. Reddy.) Mother said something to him that was so hilarious that I burst into laughter. I rolled on my back on the floor practically screaming with laughter. And then I slowly opened my eyes without any break in consciousness. I was lying on my back in bed, my whole being vibrating with joy and bliss with the intensity of the experience. "Gee," I thought, "and I haven't even met Her yet."

* * *

Coming to Mother's darshan is an experience every seeker should have at least once. I felt so relieved when I came; there were no talks, there were no lectures, no new mental doctrine or philosophy. Just the one thing that is essential, the one thing that I wanted. The direct *action* of the Divine. And the Light. And the Silence. Mother was once asked why She does everything in silence. "Talk you can get anywhere," was Her reply. I liked everything there and started coming regularly. In the beginning I always tried to have good thoughts during darshan with the result that all my bad qualities and low thoughts would come forth. Little by little I learned not to try to be anything special. Just to be still and let Mother take care of the rest.

* * *

In spring 1992, I had the opportunity to stay in Mother's house in Langgasse whenever I came to Thalheim. So little by little I got to see Mother more even outside darshan. It opened a new world for me together with new possibilities. I spent lots of time in helping with the construction work. Whenever I was in Mother's house and I had a chance, my favourite pastime would be just watching Her. I loved to watch and follow all the subtle expressions on Her face and study the way She reacts to things and communicates with people. She is the Power that created the universe, yet She is so enormously humble. One silent expression on Her face of this indescribable humility of Hers teaches me more than all the books I've read and all the lectures I've heard. It is silent teaching in its absolute form. I must sometimes have carried my watching exercise to the extreme because I remember how Mother once gestured one of the older devotees to move and stand between Her and me to cover my view.

One thing I also have observed is that Mother treats everything – animate and inanimate – with the same incredible respect. Everything is seen as an expression of the Divine. Everything, even tools, She treats with infinite loving care. I once saw a devotee throw a hammer and it fell on the ground. "We don't do that," Mother said to him.

* * *

One of my sweetest memories is when Mother came back from India in the fall of 1992. When I came to Thalheim after Mother's return I went to Her house. She was standing in the courtyard with some devotees. I joined them. When She saw me She became still and looked directly into my eyes. I stood still. This lasted for a long, long time. Everybody felt the charged atmosphere and became silent. Then finally She lowered Her eyes with a beautiful, shyish smile on Her face. This darshan which She gave to me, a newcomer, I will never forget. My heart was filled with gratitude and love for Mother.

* * *

Mother has taught me the value of doing japa. I had always given all the importance only to meditation. I knew about japa but never felt much for it. After reading Mother's *Answers* I started doing japa on Her divine name. It totally wiped away all my mental opinions and judgements about "spiritual" and "unspiritual" and made my life into an integrated whole that was filled with Her. Sometimes I would see Mother in a very subtle way wherever I looked, the whole physical world would look like a veil and She was shining through it, or She actually was it. All the experiences that sometimes come to me, come during normal waking consciousness, not in trance. That is what makes them so real. Doing japa on Mother's name is the key. It is like eating a candy bar: you say the name with deep love in your heart and then let Her sweet taste fill you. You let it linger and then repeat the name again, as if taking another bite of the candy bar. What more could anybody ask for?

In November 1992, after I started trying japa, Mother gave me an experience that was new to me. I felt an opening within my chest (like the one you often can see in Indian pictures), and within that opening I could feel and sense infinity. When I entered that space within myself I felt the source of the whole creation there. The power that flowed from that opening into my daily life was overwhelming. Others felt it, too. I went to Finland for a weekend. There I had lunch with a friend in a vegetarian restaurant. When she sat down at my table, she immediately felt that experience and started shedding tears saying, "How good it feels to be in this." And at work, when I was having lunch, for instance, I would see all the other guests in the restaurant within myself and unconditional love would flow through me to all of them. I lived with this experience for a week and then it disappeared.

* * *

In August 1993, I had the opportunity to go to India with Mother for three weeks. Much of my time was spent helping Herbert with construction work. I also had ample opportunity to continue my favourite pastime of watching Mother and learning from the way She acts. When we arrived at Her house, people from town started coming to Her to get Her blessings. I never stop being amazed at with what humility and grace She receives them when they come and touch Her feet. The poorest sadhu and the richest businessman are all received with the same love and respect. Sometimes the house was full of people, everybody eager to see Mother. How dignified She was, like a Queen.

Madanapalle, India 1993

Being physically so close to Mother can also be hard on the ego. She is like a surgeon who operates with a laser to make the patient recover from the clutches of the ego in the shortest possible time. Once I made a stupid remark and the silent look Mother gave me made me want to sink through the floor. Again, two days before my scheduled departure, I got very hurt by something that Mother said. All my undivine qualities came up and I felt just plain lousy. I felt I had had enough for this time and waited anxiously for the departure day. When we were on the way to the airport I remembered how Mother – when She said I could come with Her – had said that I could come only for three weeks. She had known exactly my capacity already months in advance. She always gives us the exact amount we are able to receive – no more, no less – during darshan and outside darshan.

* * *

After coming home from India I went out for a run. I stumbled and fell, tearing the skin of my left knee. "No big deal," I thought. I just limped back home, washed away most of the dirt and forgot all about it. One week afterwards I suddenly felt terrible pain in my left knee. It was swollen. I could not walk. Next day with great pain I managed to take myself to a hospital to see a doctor. Something in my knee had become badly infected in a very critical place that could damage the whole knee for good. He prescribed for me two different sorts of penicillin in very high doses to take for ten days. It would take three to four days before they would have any effect, he said. The doctor turned pale when he heard that I had been to India, but I calmed him saying that I got the wound here in Stockholm. Anyway, I had taken penicillin once before and knew how it totally knocks me out, so I was a little afraid of taking it. The doctor told me to come back next day to see if he had to operate on the knee to save it.

After some hesitation I gathered all my courage and decided to call Mother in India and tell what had happened. My relief was great when Adilakshmi told me, "Yes, Mother will help you." I immediately felt that everything would be all right. My rational mind, however, thought that maybe I should also take the penicillin, just in case. It was after all a question of saving my knee. "And," Adilakshmi continued, "Mother says that if you want to, you can also take the penicillin."

When I woke up next morning, all the pain was gone, the knee wasn't swollen any more and I could walk without problems. At the hospital the doctor was amazed how all the symptoms had disappeared. This is just one of the cases where I know from my own personal experience how Mother can help us also on this material plane. She takes care of all our needs, inner and outer.

* * *

One thing I don't have yet is patience. The worst thing I know is standing in a slow-moving line. Once I had another vivid experience at night. Mother and I were talking. She told me to have more patience with my spiritual life. She said that the groundwork must first be made firm and solid. Then the realization can be built upon it. "So true," I said to myself when opening my eyes. I felt so good and secure, and happily offered my whole life into Mother's hands.

* * *

These are some of the things that have happened to me since I met Mother two and a half years ago. Mother and the Paramatman Light have taken charge of my life and made it blossom the way I could never have imagined. She doesn't talk much, She *acts*. It is almost as if I do nothing myself any more. Sometimes I feel Mother is like a huge wave and I am like a happy surfer that is carried swiftly forward by that wave. Every new day feels like a new adventure where anything could happen. My home is with Her.

27.

It "somehow" happened that I am residing in Thalheim since April 94 – in the same house in which Mother Meera started to give Darshan several years ago.

Right from the first day of my stay here I have realized, particularly during my meditation programme, an immense spiritual power accumulated in this house, excelling anything that I had experienced before, in spite of being a long term meditator and having attended many prolonged meditation courses.

It took me quite some time to become a bit adjusted to it. But this power, or rather that portion of it that I am able to experience, is still increasing. To a somewhat milder degree it accompanies me also during activity to a greater extent than what I am used to before and this additional power transforms itself into some quite practical benefits.

Sometimes during the day there are phases where this power or rather Her abstract presence gets as intensive and satisfying as it does in meditation.

After coming here a new and long awaited level of experience has opened up, both in meditation and in activity. Especially during meditation this new level is experienced in forms of more depth, more energy and more fulfilment and bliss. In a very natural way – that means without effort – the attention during meditation is more inwardly directed than it has been before and this results in an increase of inner peace, power and blissful satisfaction.

After my morning programme I feel so fresh and vital – like rejuvenated. And on the way to work as well as on the way back home the surroundings of Thalheim add their own share to that state of personal well-being. They seem to reflect the divine charm and purity of Mother Meera. The whole atmosphere around Thalheim and the neighbouring countryside radiates a particular glow of serenity, purity, and beauty. It is very pleasing to look at and so far I have not found such a sublime lustre anywhere else in Germany. People living in this area must be very blessed, even without knowing it.

During the about one-minute period of the personal Darshan I don't have any visions or spectacular experiences, except that looking into Mother Meera's eyes makes me feel very good. Her eyes are so beautiful, so pure, so awake and clear, and so full of knowledge and they express compassion as well as complete detachment. It is like becoming satisfied after a very long craving for something that cannot easily be formulated.

Sometimes, however, when my intellect happens to be more quiet – that is, when I don't try to analyse or to understand what is going on during Darshan – then I have a subtle feeling of lightness and exaltation. But the moment it reaches its highest point and makes me want to grab it then the Darshan is over...

Also during the short period of sitting on the waiting chair in the immediate vicinity of Mother Meera, I rejoice in a kind of wave of bliss-power that surrounds Her or is radiating from Her. And when after the Darshan I sit down for meditation, then there is a burst of this bliss and power in my mind and body. And this goes on or starts anew when sitting down for meditation at home, before going to bed, and it continues during the programme next morning.

One practical benefit of staying here and therefore of bathing in the grace of Mother Meera is that the need for sleep has become less. And that is not only due to the fact of living in the calmness of the countryside, away from the city life, but because of the harmony and the high degree of order radiated by Mother Meera, which enriches the quality of the whole environment.

Also it happens frequently, more frequently than only chance would allow, that for example on the way to work I read exactly those parts which are needed that day for doing my job. I have had a lot of other surprising coincidences as well since I came here, which somehow give the feeling of life being well guided.

This statement can be valued only after shortly explaining that my job is to give special help in mathematics and physics at a private institution and that before I came to Thalheim and started working there I had not done any mathematics or physics for more than a decade with the result that my knowledge about these topics was almost zero – in some cases it was even below the level of the children I am teaching.

But surprisingly enough within a comparatively short time I could brush up quite a lot of this knowledge and moreover I like it the same way it fascinated me at the time I was a student. This is in itself another very surprising event for me, because my studies lie back almost 15 years and at that time I was literally no more able to focus on topics of modern science. There was simply not even a bit of energy or creativity left for it. I did not even want to look at books of physics or mathematics, nor was I able to read or study them, although these two topics had formerly been the central part of my life. Probably this was due to my overexerting myself during the long years of study as well as to the fact that Nature had put me into a completely different form of existence, starting with my initiation into spiritual life about 17 years ago. Ever since only spiritual matters would wake my interest and concern, to the exclusion of everything else. Some years later spirituality had even become my profession with which I earned my livelihood. The pendulum had shifted to the far end of the opposite side – from an almost purely rational way of thinking and living to spirituality (as I wanted to understand it those days). Finally of course spirituality does not exclude the objective realm of life, but in fact enriches it since spirituality is the very basis of life. Although I had this understanding I still had to go through my particular experiences as indicated above, before I was able to accept this – that is before I could practically live it.

Now, after all these years when my way of living had been determined by predominantly using the intuitive side of the brain I find myself in the very surprising situation of being able to make use of the analytical side again, but now together with the intuitive side. Again I am getting fascinated by he subjects of my former study so that now I can combine them with spirituality in a very fulfilling way. In this way both the spiritual and practical aspects of my life have become harmonized and I find myself in a process of integration.

For me the only explanation for what is happening is Mother Meera's organizing power with which She is reorganizing everything and everybody and putting it or them at the right place – like a gardener cultivating the beet.

How I came to know Mother Meera

The first time I heard about Mother Meera was in 1983 when I joined a permanent international spiritual group stationed in Germany. In the room of one of the group members I saw a black and white photograph of Mother Meera. He said to me that this was Mother Meera, a holy person from India, living in a small village at the other side of the river Rhein. At that time my mind was not open for other spiritual directions so I decided to forget about it, although now and then other group members talked to me about Her.

Three years later another group member invited me one evening to a Puja (a ceremony of gratitude to the Masters or the spiritual tradition of Masters). There was also a photo of Mother Meera on the Puja table. The photo was beautiful, really captivating. It gave me something, some-thing very precious. There were also many other photos of Mother Meera in the room. During the Puja I felt kind of elated, unmistakingly more than on other occasions, also afterwards but especially the next morning during the programme. I felt very blissful and this continued during the day.

That group member then inspired me to attend a Darshan with Mother Meera. I decided to go there since I took my good experiences during and after the Puja as a kind of invitation to come to Darshan. Still it took me a long time until I was really ready to go because I did not want to cause a break to my spiritual line. The night after the first Darshan I had a dream which released me from that doubt. I understood that there is no conflict at all in having the Darshan of Mother Meera

189

while belonging to a different spiritual line, for both of them are working together in total harmony, although each of them has a different approach or method of uplifting mankind.

That doubt did not come back any more. And especially after moving to Thalheim I realized that a doubt of this kind is only due to a limited understanding of life. Eventually life is one integral, timeless, all-pervading wholeness, so different manifestations of that abstract Entity, that underlies everything, cannot really act against each other. However, from the perspective of the incomplete human beings it may appear to be so.

But now I feel good where I am. There is no feeling of having taking an inadequate step nor is there a feeling of guiltiness with regard to my previous spiritual tradition. Instead there is the assurance from within that Mother Meera has put me at the right place at the right time. Actually I feel really relaxed and freed – freed from my own stubbornness which for the last 15 years has caused me to look upon life from a rather one-sided perspective.

An excellent teaching

Right from the beginning when I came to know Mother Meera I felt a very pure and deep but yet kind of personal love for Her. It was the beauty of Her physical appearance and the Purity that She radiates that dominated the attraction I felt towards Her.

Then during one of the first Darshans I received the following excellent teaching from Her. The teaching was excellent because of the way it was imparted to me and because of its contents and because of its effect on me. It was communicated to me without talking, solely through the power of silence: "I am not the body but Pure Consciousness. And even if I would be physically near you you would not have attained Me. Therefore, strive to realize Me to be Pure Consciousness."

Ever since I am trying to get a more and more abstract understanding of what She really is. I am very grateful for this teaching, which I remember even today exactly as it was given to me.

* * *

Credit for all the good that we are graciously offered by Mother Meera, irrespectively whether one stays here in the vicinity or elsewhere, goes also to Adilakshmi who always cheers up Mother's devotees by her radiant, very sympathetic and cordial smile and her rich and matured personality, making the devotees feel welcome and at home when they come to Darshan. Seeing Adilakshmi, especially on those not so frequent occasions outside Darshan, is really like an extra blessing.

In this regard I would like to add one very pleasing experience with Adilakshmi. One morning when I was doing asanas Adilakshmi came over and asked me to do a job. It took her less than 30 seconds to explain the job for me. Afterwards I resumed my asanas and then felt as if given shaktipat (transfer of spiritual energy). There was a strong enchantment of bliss in the whole body as if she had imparted to me a portion of that divine Shakti which she constantly receives from Mother Meera, carrying it with her and radiating it to the devotees.

So I am happy here, feeling really at home. The reward that one receives from Mother Meera for being open-minded and willing to the process of transformation that She carries out by bringing down the light of Paramatman, is freedom and peace, growing inner contentment, bliss, power, and joy.

28.

(Ten years old:) Two years ago I had holidays in Mother's house, together with my parents and my brother. It was a time I will never forget. We played very much and all was beautiful. Best was to be with Mother upstairs in her flat. I cannot yet understand that it was so wonderful there. We never did very much, but it was never boring. Time passed away rapidly. The Mother was there, and it was nice.

Sometimes Mother went for a walk with us. Once we went to the samadhi of Mr. Reddy. Mother watered the flowers with us. Subsequently we went with Mother to a playground. That was very funny.

Mother's garden was always a joy for us, especially at the time when strawberries were ripening. We picked and ate them. When we met Mother in the house she almost every time had a small or a big surprise for us. Often delicate sweets or once a tea-set for puppets. I still like to play with it. A suitcase of bast was a gift of Mother. I always take it with me, on all journeys.

But my most wonderful experience was this: One day we all went to the airport of Frankfurt to see Adilakshmi off. It took a long time because the plane was late. Nevertheless it was fine because we sat with Mother in the waiting-hall talking. Afterwards we were allowed to drive back in Mother's car. Meanwhile I had become sleepy and my eyes were closing. Now, Mother took my head on her lap and I fell asleep. My sleep was so marvelous that I will never forget it. To live in Mother's house is wonderful.

Also, Mother helps me if there is a problem. Usually I am not anxious. Once there was a situation with great fear. I wrote a letter to Mother and told her all. Immediately all was well. I could forget fear.

Again and again I like to go to Mother. There it is beautiful. Sometimes I think the drive is too long because I don't like to drive too long. But when I am back home after Darshan I feel so good. I can be tired before Darshan, but I am wide awake and fresh afterwards. The silence I feel after Darshan is very comfortable. Oh, there is one more thing. On the journey to Thalheim I don't notice the landscape. But on return it is beautiful every time.

I am grateful to Mother that I can always come to Her.

29.

(Twelve years old:) Spending holidays in Mother's house with my family was an amazing experience. There I felt very comfortable. It was the first time anywhere, that I felt better than at home. Mother's house was my home during all the time of holidays. Every time we got back from an adventure I thought: "Now, I am coming home."

Actually I never felt like departing from there. Most beautiful was talking with Mother or going along with her. All was marvelous with Mother. Even only walking or going to Mr. Reddy's samadhi was fascinating.

And, Mother always had a surprise for us: delicious sweets or once Mother gave me a dredge machine for playing, very beautiful.

Often Mother brought us vegetables from her own garden for cooking. Usually I don't like vegetables. But I still know that the beans from Mother's garden tasted SUPER!

Thalheim, Germany 1984

Mother also allowed us to take photos. They are all beautiful and I keep them in a special album.

Well, something I couldn't understand at all. Normally I'm not willing to work. Sometimes Mother gave me something to do. And what did I find out? That even this was pleasant.

When I think of those holidays I know it was the most wonderful thing I have ever experienced. After that we were often allowed to spend weekends in Mother's house. I am always looking forward to these unforgettable events.

Mother always helped when I had any problems. There was a time in school when I did not want to learn. Everything felt heavy and difficult. After Mother came to know about it all got better, like a miracle. School was pleasant and examination marks good again.

When I had just become ten years old I asked Mother for permission to come to Darshan. I can still remember my first Darshan. It was almost three years ago. I was still a bit uncertain whether to sit on the waiting chair. I sat down. After Darshan when I was going back to my place all sorrows and problems disappeared. Even today it is still remaining this way.

When I am in Darshan it is very silent. In this silence I can think over many things. After each Darshan I feel better. If it weren't for the long drive, I would like to have Darshan four times a week. Every Monday I look forward to Friday when we will again drive to Darshan.

I am very glad about Mother being in Germany and allowing me to come to Darshan.

30.

Since I do not have the eyes of wisdom, I do not know who Mother is or what she is. But in her I have found a caring, gentle Master who will guide me on my journey Home.

It has been a long and arduous journey for me so far to come to Mother. Though I was unaware at the time, my childhood and the rich tradition I was brought up in had prepared me well for this pilgrimage. I grew up in the Tiruchirappalli area of Southern India, an area famous for its majestic temples, rich culture and and long tradition. My parents are ardent devotees of the Divine Mother that had rubbed off on me quite a bit from my childhood. My paternal grandmother was a living encyclopedia of the Hindu legends, lore and mythology. She served me every meal with fascinating stories of gods and goddesses. Through her I also learned that the way to pray is to take refuge at the feet of God and hold on to His feet. Little did I realize at that time that I would eventually do exactly that with Mother Meera.

Graduate school brought me to the United States in the early seventies. I not only imbibed the latest advances in science and technology, but also had a quick fill of material comforts and pleasures. I quickly learned that they did not provide lasting happiness. At the same time, I was also questioning and even rebelling against religious concepts, including that of God and the way I had understood and practiced religion.

It was my good fortune that I came across *The Gospel of Sri Ramakrishna* and *The Bhagavad Gita*. *The Gospel* was an eye-opener to me that God can actually be realized and that is the sole purpose of life. Sri Ramakrishna's devotion to the Divine Mother appealed very much to me since I had prayed to Her all my childhood and youth albeit for temporal things ranging from relief from childhood diseases such as chicken pox to getting top grades in school. *The Bhagavad Gita* exposed me to the philosophical aspects of religion. Many verses in the Gita tallied with my psychological experience and observations of life.

God-realization soon became a passion for me and I read a lot and was fortunate to have had the blessings of a few Mahatmas whom I kept in touch with and who inspired me much in my spiritual practice.

A few years ago, I had come across a short note on Mother Meera, an Indian lady saint living in Germany. The article struck a chord in me and I tucked it away in a corner of my memory. However, I did not act on it for I was not the type who rushed to visit a saint the moment I read an article. If I was really turned on, it typically took me several months to get a few books and read up and often a few more years for me to go and see the saint if I felt I would gain spiritually. It was also my notion at that time that a Mahatma worth his or her deer skin must live in India running an ashram.

Now, reflecting on Mother's residence in Germany, I'd rather have her stay in Germany than in India. Of course, USA would be even better.

The airfare to Germany is about half of that to India so Rani (my wife) and I don't have to argue who gets to visit Mother and who doesn't. We both can see Mother for the price of one air ticket to India. If we add the costs of all the gifts we buy for our trip to India, and the items we bring back from India, we are looking at something as expensive as an Indian parent marrying his daughter off.

It is also easier to sneak in a weekend trip to Germany while visits to India need at least a month if I want to stay on the good side of my parents, in-laws, relatives and friends. Considering my penchant for pilgrimages to Mahatmas, temples, and ashrams, one month is barely enough. For these reasons, I would certainly prefer to have Mother in Germany than in India.

In early summer of 1993, Rani Ramachandran, children Purna and Anand and I were travelling to Seattle, Washington. We had stopped overnight at a friend's house in Portland, Oregon, where we saw a picture of Mother Meera. The moment my eyes fell on the picture, I was very much drawn to her and the old memories of the article surfaced to the conscious level. The friend showed me the book *Answers* by Mother Meera. Thumbing through the book my eyes fell on the picture of Mother on page 86. I was captivated by the beauty of her eyes that reminded of the eyes of Bhagavan Sri Ramana Maharishi. Sri Ramana had been a spiritual beacon in my life. That picture of Mother continues to thrill me even today.

I also finished reading *Answers* before we left for Seattle next morning. I found Mother Meera's answers spontaneous and pertinent and her replies quite modern in outlook and sympathetic to the householder's predicament of balancing his or her spiritual aspirations with wordly responsibilities.

Intrigued by the book, I ordered a copy of *Answers* on our return to San Jose. I kept thinking about her and a desire to see her was growing stronger. I first wanted to visit her in August of 1993 but it didn't work out. I also unsuccesfully tried to visit her in October and then in December on my way to India.

Rani went to see Mother in January of 1994 immediately after my return from India. While she was in Germany, one day I woke up in the middle of the night feeling a very strong presence of Mother Meera. I noted the time and went back to sleep. Next day, Rani excitedly called me about her being in Mother's house and the exchange she was having with Mother through Adilakshmi. Getting very curious, I asked her what time she had visited Mother and was certainly awestruck that it coincided with the time I had noted down. Later, when I narrated this incident to Mother, she nodded as if in agreement.

Rani returned from Germany visibly touched and rejuvenated. Rani had brought a picture of Mother from Thalheim. She framed it and kept it on the altar in our puja (worship) room.

We had converted the third car garage in our house into a puja room and we had to pass by its door when we went into the garage. I often found myself opening the puja room door and looking at Mother's picture or sitting in front of the altar when I was in the garage.

Thoughts of Mother were with me when I was driving since I spent considerable time on the road. I went to bed thinking about her and woke up with thoughts of her. Even before Rani had returned from Germany, I had written a note to Mother and Adilakshmi thanking them for their solicitude toward Rani. That was only the beginning of numerous letters I wrote to Mother through Adilakshmi. In the beginning, it was a trickle, a letter a month, and soon it became a flood with with a frequency of almost once a week and sometimes more often. To me letter writing normally had the same level of appeal and excitement as paying bills and balancing the check book. As such, even I was amazed at the spontaneity and frequency of my lettters.

In Summer of '94, I had a strong desire to get a copy of *The Mother* by Adilakshmi. The Meeramma Publication in New York had told me earlier that the book was out of print. So I wrote a letter to Adilakshmi asking whether I could borrow her copy, read it and return it to her. Unbeknownst to her, Adilakshmi had written us a note saying she was sending us two copies of the new edition of *The Mother*. We were eagerly and impatiently awaiting the book. A few weeks later a packet arrived and in it were two copies with one copy blessed by Mother and signed by Adilakshmi.

After a few days of soul searching and weighing the pros and cons, I agreed with Rani that it was best to travel together in October. We also picked a weekend that coincided with Dasara (a ten day worship of Divine Mother and celebration of Her victory over evil) and also with my birthday. We duly apprised Adilakshmi of our new plans. She readily agreed and much to our delight invited us to stay at Mother's house.

We hit a few snags before our trip in the matters of our reservations and arrangements for our children who were staying behind. Frantic phone calls and prayers to Mother eventually solved the problems and we were all set.

Rani and I started for Frankfurt from San Francisco on Thursday, October 13, 1994, and arrived at Mother's house on Friday morning. I was very happy to meet Adilakshmi for the first time. She showed us to our room. After familiarizing us with the room she left us to rest.

The room was in another part of Mother's house. Mother's house is in the shape of an 'L' with Mother living on the third floor of the base of the 'L'. Our room was on the vertical leg of the 'L' and was on the second floor. Access to Mother's part of the house was through an open balcony that led to the stairwell in the main part of the house. This gives Mother the much needed privacy while the guests can also come and go as they please without disturbing the residents of the house.

Adilakshmi came to our room around 6:15 PM to take us to the darshan hall. After showing us our seats, she went to greet devotees arriving for darshan. If Mother Meera is the spiritual mother of seekers coming for her darshan, Adilakshmi is the 'big sister' of Mother's family. She was genuinely interested in everyone coming to see Mother and wanted to make sure he or she was comfortably seated. This often meant squeezing in one or two extra persons on the floor so that they can get a good view of Mother.

Visitors started arriving around 6:30 PM and the hall was buzzing with people greeting each other, finding a seat, and settling down. Within about fifteen minutes or so, a soft and soothing silence fell over the room with everyone meditating or silently anticipating Mother's entry. At 7:00 PM sharp, Mother entered the hall and Rani and I were very thrilled to see Mother wearing the silk sari we had brought for her. We were very touched that Mother chose to wear it in the first place and that too on the very first day of our darshan.

The darshan started and I noticed that Mother's way of giving darshan was the same for everyone yet it was ever fresh. Even though the entire darshan lasted about over two hours, I never felt that it was long. There was a palpable peace in the room and I wished the darshan would last longer.

It was a little humbling and also much inspiring to me to see the devotees in the darshan hall. Most of them were Westerners who had grown up in a culture where the concept of Divine Mother or Self-realization must have been very alien. Yet, I could feel the intensity of their devotion in the hall and was very impressed by the reverence and humility with which they approached Mother for darshan and sat in the hall in absolute silence and stillness for over two hours.

After darshan that evening, and every evening we were there, we spent another hour or so with Adilakshmi who shared with us events and memories of her family, her life with Mother, Mr. Reddy and Mother's devotees.

We were too excited to sleep that night and were concerned that we may oversleep. The time difference between California and Frankfurt was eight hours and we were suffering from acute jet-lag. I found the jet-lag actually a blessing since every night I would stay awake most of the night thinking about Mother, recollecting the darshan, what to write or tell her and so on. It was a wonderful form of sadhana (spiritual practice) for me.

Saturday was very special for us. It was the Vijayadasami day, the last day of the ten day worship of the Divine Mother. It was also my birthday. On this day, we went to Mother's room. Mother was dressed in a green sari with a matching turquoise sweater. We did our prostration and sat at her feet on the floor along with Adilakshmi. I had made a long list of supplications which I started reeling off to Mother. After a while I found it somewhat disconcerting that I was carrying on a monologue while Mother had remained silent throughout except for an occasional nod or smile. I was looking for reassurances and affirmations but none came forth. However, after some time when we specifically asked her questions and guidance on personal and spiritual matters, she was kind enough to give specific answers. They were sound and practical. Rani also used the occasion to discuss a problem that has been vexing us for long. While Rani and I agreed on all major issues both spiritual and temporal, there was one spiritual issue that was an irritant in our marriage since we were poles apart on this matter. Mother told us that dispassion (vairagya) could not be forced upon and would come in due course of time. She also told us that we had to live in this world and carry out our activities.

We had brought a gift – a complete Indian set of golden jewellery – for Mother. She wanted us to take it back as her blessing. After much remonstration, she accepted it. However, she returned our checks that we had sent as our offerings over a period of time. Rani and I had always felt that it was our duty as householders to serve holy persons. Mother said we had children who needed the money for their education and other needs and we should keep it. On this matter, no amount of persuasion could change her mind and we had to reluctantly take back all our checks.

After that evening's darshan I felt a great peace that lasted the entire next day. I usually did japa (repetition of God's name) whenever I became aware my mind was wandering. That day I could not do japa even when I wanted to, yet the mind was still. The third day's darshan was perhaps what I enjoyed the most. Everyday, I was fortunate to have a seat in the back of the room almost directly facing Mother. From this vantage point, I could see her eyes and drink in the charm and the grace of darshan as the looked into the devotee's eyes. On this day, I was very much captivated by the way she held the devotee's head between her hands. I was feeling a subtle current of her energy flowing in me. That feeling lasted the entire darshan. Our visit also had its painful moments. My heart felt quite heavy and sad on the last day of darshan that I would not be seeing the physical form of Mother until she willed it again and I would have to carry on my sadhana with whatever energy and faith she had infused in me. Even now, I feel the anguish that I could not see her often or serve her physically.

Rani and I are deeply indebted to Adilakshmi who was instrumental in strengthening our ties to Mother. She was a very gracious hostess on behalf of Mother and was ever attentive to make sure our stay was comfortable. She would visit us in our room and made us very happy by sharing her experiences. The day before we left, she gave us two large boxes of candies blessed by Mother and a jar of jam made by Mother and Adilakshmi from strawberries grown in Mother's garden. We were extremely touched to receive those. We shared the candies with many of our friends who also felt very happy to receive the prasad (blessing) from Mother though they have not been devotees themselves. I told Adilakshmi that in my visit to Germany I had not only gained a spiritual Mother but also a spiritual 'big sister'. Adilakshmi also felt that I reminded her of her late brother and shared several traits with him. Of course, it was not all serious or spiritual. There were many lighter conversations also. Adilakshmi would assure Rani that Indian men are not very expressive, but deep down they have great love for their wives.

Even after our return home, I still have strong recollections of Mother and feel that my spiritual ties to her have become stronger. The strong sense of peace I had felt in Thalheim comes to me involuntarily occasionally. Whatever life may bring, I know I can call on Mother for succor and feel secure in her care. I pray that she will help me develop one-pointedness and guide me to the Goal. More than anything else, to quote from *The Gospel of Sri Ramakrishna*, may she fulfill my longing:

"Oh, Mother, make me mad with Thy love
What need I have of knowledge or reasoning . . ."

31.

I was born in an orthodox, brahmin family and grew up in a very spiritual town in South India. I still remember my mother getting up early morning and doing her japa and my brothers learning Vedas when I was a little girl. To be very honest, nothing really appealed to me and I used to rebel with my parents for making me participate in religious activities. I grew up to be a very wordly person with not much interest in religion or spirituality. Going to a catholic school further confused my views on spirituality. My marriage to Ram was a turning point in my life. I did not know then but I know it now. Our marriage was arranged by our parents and we met just a few days before our marriage. Ram used to constantly talk about God and spirituality which I was never able to comprehend or understand. Immediately after marriage, and in the following years, I accompanied him to see many saints on a regular basis. He also frequently told me interesting stories about them. Very slowly I started showing interest in some of the things he told me and eventually I enjoyed visiting saints with him. My life, both professional as a doctor and personal, has been a roller coaster which also forced me to turn to the Divine. I guess Mother was preparing me to meet her at the right time.

In the summer of 1993 we visited our friend in Portland, Oregon who showed us a picture of Mother Meera and an interesting article about her. Both Ram Ramachandran and I were immediately attracted to her. Eventually we bought the book *Answers* and Mother impressed me with her simple down to earth answers for complicated questions. Ram wanted to see her right away but somehow I was resistant to his seeing her without me. The next few months I was caught up in our day to day activities and just did not think about Mother Meera a whole lot. Around the Christmas of 1993, I ended up having many stresses professionally. My desire to go and see Mother became stronger and stronger. Unlike me, Ram was very willing to help me to go to Germany alone. Fortunately, we have never had any financial trouble to go on pilgrimages. Ram went through the process of calling Mother's house and told Bernd that I wanted to come the following week and that was the only time I could take off from work. Unfortunately, there was no reservation available for me to visit Mother. Both Ram and I were very disappointed and I was trying to put away the thoughts of going to Germany. I felt I had seen many saints in my life and perhaps this was not the right time for me to see Mother. Right after his call, Ram suggested that I call Germany myself to try my luck and he left for work. Reluctantly, I called around 8 A.M., California time. I was surprised when Adilakshmi answered the phone and I explained the situation to her. She told me to come any time I could. My heart was filled with joy; I was destined to see Mother after all. I immediately wrote a letter to Mother for the first time and got ready to see her the following week. I was still wondering in my mind whether this was worth spending all this money in going to Germany.

The following week, I called Adilakshmi to reconfirm my plans to visit Mother. I asked her what I could bring for Mother and she replied, "You bring an empty cup and Mother will fill it with Love." How true was her statement! It was Pongal (thanksgiving after harvest) time and my brother had sent me a beautiful silk sari for me as per Indian tradition. Somehow, I felt I should take it for Mother as I had seen her wear beautiful saris in the photographs. The first day of darshan did not have much impression on me. I had been used to totally different way of darshan. But I did feel something different inside of me.

After the first day of darshan I expressed my desire to speak to Adilakshmi. She at once invited me to come to Mother's house the following morning. I had a list of things to ask of Mother. Adilakshmi patiently took all my messages to Mother and came back with direct answers for all my questions and most of them were very personal. All my problems seemed very minimal to me and I felt I could easily face them. Mother also autographed a photo of hers for my 8 year old son which my son had wanted. After my delightful conversation with

Mother and Adilakshmi I decided to take a bus back to the hotel though I did not have the address nor had any clue as to how I could get back to the hotel. But somehow nothing mattered to me any more at that particular time. The weather was very cold and I had gone to Mr. Reddy's samadhi when someone from Mother's house came and gave me a ride to the hotel. I then realized how Mother pays attention to even small details.

From then on, all I could think about was Mother and her sweetness. I was looking forward to the evening darshan. I was more peaceful and calm and I was crying a lot in joy for the next three days. I was often constantly thinking about Mother and I kept calling Ram in California every few hours to tell him how happy I was. The last darshan day was very special to me. When I entered Mother's house Adilakshmi jokingly told me to have a lot of tissues to wipe off my tears. When Mother walked into the darshan room in the sari I had brought for Mother, I could not resist my tears any more. She looked dazzling in the sari and I could not stop crying at her kindness in wearing the sari. Mother is above and beyong expecting any gifts from anyone but she accepts them to make us happy. What can I say. I then knew that I had found my divine Mother.

I returned to USA and my thoughts of Mother were constant. I was getting less upset about things. I was able to handle my job stresses more effeciently. At time of difficulty, I always looked at Mother and the thought of her filler me with comfort. Any time I thought about Mother, my eyes were filled with tears of joy. I knew I could turn to her for any of my problems. Slowly we got connected to Mother more and more. Adilakshmi invited all of us to come and stay at Mother's house during our next visit. In the next few months Ram had some stomach problems and he needed surgical intervention. Mother said that she would take care of him. The procedure went very well and Ram has been free of this problem so far though medically there is a good chance of recurrence.

We visited Mother again in October 1994. Mother and Adilakshmi showered their love on us. We spent about 40 minutes in Mother's presence. She spoke very little but was looking at us with love and affection. When we asked specific questions she always had a very practical and straightforward answer. Though I had been strongly convinced she is my Divine Mother I often had doubts about her. When I expressed this to Mother, she comforted me by saying it is very natural to have doubts and in a way it has a positive effect on our faith.

Thalheim, Germany 1984

During our stay, I offered to cook for Mother one day which she very graciously accepted. I was very happy and made a few dishes for her. After Mother had eaten, Adilakshmi brought us the rest of the food as Mother's prasad. She said Mother liked my Sambar (a South Indian dish, prepared with vegetables and pulses, and usually eaten with rice). Mother gave us a bottle of strawberry jam to take with us. Our children who do not usually like to eat jam, love it a lot and they keep saying the jar should grow full so that they can have it every day.

On the day of our departure, Adilakshmi spent a lot of time with us. We accompanied her to Mr. Reddy's samadhi where we helped her to tidy up the samadhi and offer flowers. I prayed to Mother to give me devotion like Mr. Reddy had towards her.

I feel I have a true mother-child relationship with Mother Meera. I ask her for just about everything, little and big, spiritual and mundane. Mother patiently listens to everything like a real mother. Whenever I come across difficulty or mental restlessness, I read *The Mother* and *Answers* which give me comfort and peace.

I am not a person of wisdom. I do make a lot of mistakes in my life. I also waste my precious time in unwanted things. I am very fortunate to have known Mother. I know she will lead me in the right path. Whatever life has to offer me I know I can turn to my loving Mother for help and guidance.

"O Mother, owing to my ignorance of the injunctions relating to my worship, as also owing to my laziness I had not the power to do what I ought to have done; so, O Mother, Auspicious One, Deliverer of all, whatever faults of omission I might have committed, forgive me, for a bad child may sometimes be born, but there is never a bad Mother."[1] This is my constant prayer to Mother Meera.

32.

(*Eleven years old:*) I have two very special Divine Mothers. Each of them is the very essence of love. Both of them are the most Supreme beings in the world.

[1] From Sri Shankara's "A Hymn to the Divine Mother Craving Forgiveness", Altar Flowers, Advaita Ashrama, 1968.

But I'm only going to talk about one: the Divine Mother I have never met, Mother Meera. I have come to know about her through my mom. It all started when our friends in Oregon told us about her. My parents received a book from them and a picture of her. They were very impressed with the book.

My mom decided to go to Germany. She really liked Mother Meera. After that we started to write to Mother Meera. This October both of my parents went to Germany. I made an art work for Mother Meera and my parents gave it to her. Adilakshmi told them that Mother liked it. My parents brought back special experiences and gifts from Mother. The gifts were wonderful, strawberry jam from the garden and made by Mother, hoards of German chocolate, medallions for each member of my family, and the most wonderful gift of all, love and best wishes from the Mother.

Dearest Mother, I thank you for giving me your blessings for the spelling bee. I did get very far thanks to your grace. I thank you so much. If it weren't for you I wouldn't be in the position I am right now. I had won $100 in the regional spelling bee and I am planning to give you half of the money for donation. I hope you will accept this small token offered to you with my love.

Like I said before, I have two very special Mothers and that is one thing no one can take away from me.

33.

When I came to Thalheim for the first time I wanted to learn from Mother Meera how to die. I was in my 80th year, distressed by the increasing feebleness of my body with its many aches and anxieties. I wanted her to help me slip painlessly into a benign death.

But Mother didn't see my situation that way at all. On the contrary, she completely turned my expectations around. And my life as well.

On the night of my first darshan in May of 1993 I came to the hall with some fear and trembling. Not only was I awed by Mother's reputation. I also bore a long-standing distrust of the wisdom of mothers. My own mother, born of Prussian parents, had been a punishing and unforgiving parent. Her response to my spiritual aspirations took the form of indifference or chastisement. I had to find my own path to self-acceptance and to the life of the spirit. Through the years I sought the counsel of priests, gurus, philosophers, and therapists. I prayed fervently to Jesus, Shiva and Buddha. I never experienced grace from a goddess, no matter how often I hailed the Virgin Mary.

When I first knelt in front of Mother's chair, I was stunned by her beauty and serene power. In a shimmering gold sari, arms folded and eyes lowered, she looked like a delicate but magnanimous queen of heaven. I was immediately convinced that she came from another world. I lowered my head for her to hold as she examined my soul. At her touch a shudder went through me that I shall always remember. I knew in that moment that my life would never be the same.

I asked her in my heart to ease my bodily disintegration. Her reply to this was to illuminate the true state of my being. With one stroke of her shakti light she punctured my fear of death and dying. She showed me how I was not fatally ill nor permanently crippled. I was simply too identified with the agonies of ageing. I had not been aware how my soul was still ageless and still bubbling. This accurate clarification unsettled me. Removal of the worries that I had clung to left me feeling stranded. But Mother wasted no time in filling the emptiness she had put me in.

At my second darshan when she looked deeply into my eyes, she zipped open my heart. It spilled forth all my bottled-up feelings, all the sorrows and longings and mistakes of my life. By the time I got back to my seat I had begun to weep uncontrollably. I covered my face to stifle my sobbing.

Most of all I was flooded with intense compassion for all those close to me throughout my life whom I had not loved enough or whom I had taken for granted: my children, their mother, my own mother, lost friends and lovers and cohorts. In that moment I wanted to make it up to all of them.

This shock of recognition also made me aware of other insensitive blunders I had been guilty of. I began then to understand what karma is. This alarmed me. I hoped that my third darshan would prove more soothing. But Mother can be relentless once you have surrendered your hopes to her.

Having clarified my vision and forced open my heart she next aimed for my ego. This she did in a quite enigmatic manner. That evening when I rose from her presence and went back to my chair I was puzzled to hear myself repeating: "I am not here any more. I am not here any more." Did that mean that I was already dead, or on my way to the grave? That I was not in my right mind? That I was not living in true reality?

This koan haunted my sleep. By dawn I thought I could understand what Mother was telling me. I am not here any more because I am no longer the person I thought I was, no longer the person I was before Mother emptied my heart. I had been taken somewhere different than I had ever been. Now I had to find out where that was.

The next night when I knelt before her I asked Mother to reveal to me what I most needed in my life to heal my doubts and despairs. As she looked into me with her warm penetrating eyes I felt shafts of divine love shooting from them. They were not mortal eyes, they belonged to God. Once I was back in my seat I heard clearly: "All you need is the Divine." This repeated again and again: "All you need is the Divine."

This was so direct, so obvious, so clear an answer. I felt great relief, as if a long-closed window had been opened on a meadow of redemption. But the words challenged me. How could I bring the Divine into my everyday behavior, how to bring reverence and sublimity into everything I do and wherever I go?

I heard myself saying: "All I *want* is the Divine." And who was the Divine but Mother Meera? Wasn't she the direct connection to enlightenment? So I began to say: "All I need is Mother Meera." I vowed absolute loyalty to her henceforth with all the love my heart could summon. With her help I could hope to enter that secret meadow of redemption that she had revealed to my soul.

When my partner Joel Singer and I returned to our home in the state of Washington, we decided to consecrate a room in our house as a sanctuary for Mother. We painted the entire room gold, installed a plum-colored carpet, and put shoji screens on the windows. We erected an altar of purple hardwood which we decorated with plants, candles and incense, plus images of dancing Shiva, St. Francis with birds, and Our Lady of Mercy. Over the altar we hung an enlarged portrait of Mother framed in gold and draped with a snake skin shed by a friend's pet python.

This has become the most precious room in our house, and the most potent. We are deeply comforted to have Mother living with us in her own room. We visit her daily for japa, prayer and praises. In return she blesses us with light, insight and unfailing love.

We came again to Thalheim for Mother's 33rd birthday at Christmas time in 1993. That night she looked especially regal and radiant in an orange-pink sari dappled with tiny clusters of pale green flowers. I was struck once more by her transcendent beauty. I wanted to cry out to her: "I love you! I love you!" She did not look much like the photograph I had been praying to for six months at home. I realized that no camera can truly capture the mystery of her presence.

On that celebration of her birth I asked her again about my death. She counseled me not to worry about the eventuality of it. She urged me to respect the stresses of old age, not resent them. Since I was "still growing in my soul" I was not about to perish. Only when one stops "growing" does one die.

In return I asked Mother how I could help her work of waking the world to the glory and joy of the Divine. I have put my life completely into her hands and I want to do whatever she asks of me. I am so grateful that after many long years I could discover in the flesh a supreme mother who does not scold and punish but accepts me with unconditional sympathy and love. Praise and thanks, praise and thanks. I hope I can grow up enough to become at last her very own child.

A Gift from the Mother

Come to me as my godchild.
I am your immortal mother
disguised as a mortal being.
I am here to heal your woes
and hearten your hopes.
I am here to gladden you
with unconditional love.

Whatever you have done or will do
whatever secrets burden you
I welcome you as you are.
I do not preach or campaign.
My compassion is free to all.
I offer you a supreme light
to liberate the light in you.

This potent light can free
all who dwell in the dark.
And it is always available.
Ask for it anywhere at any time.
Offer your sorrows to it
embrace its radiance
and let it transform your life.

All depends on your aspiration
and your trust in the Divine.
To bless your days with joy
is my reason for being on the earth.
Aspire to your inevitable bliss
and every grace will be given you.
This is my solemn promise.

34.

In 1980 while we were living in Sri Lanka I was awakened one morning before dawn. I sat up in bed and through the gauzy white mosquito netting saw a woman at the foot of the bed. I recognized Jenny my nanny and surrogate mother of my early childhood years. She wore an elaborate golden headdress. She blessed me in silence, smiled benevolently and vanished. A few weeks later I received a letter from my sister telling me that Jenny (who had raised her as well) had died.

On a spring day in 1985 a few friends and I spent the day on a remote beach in Northern California. I walked off alone to explore the area and suddenly found myself being drawn by a strong force to a seated figure a few hundred yards away. As I approached her I noticed Her head was wrapped in a beautiful shawl. I went over to Her and sat in the sand directly in front of Her. She placed Her hands on my forehead and temples and silently blessed me. I knew I was in the presence of the Divine Mother. Later that evening after spending the day in silence I spoke with my friend about how he had appeared to me as the Divine Mother. He had been fully aware that he had merged with the Mother who was blessing me through him.

These two silent encounters were to prepare me for the ultimate experience of Mother Meera's Darshan which I first received in the fall of 1991. Before deciding to make the pilgrimage to Thalheim I had a dream in which Mother appeared and invited me into Her house. I made plans to go as soon as I could.

My heart was about to leap out of my chest as I sat in the waiting chair the night of my first Darshan. I was terrified and wildly excited but when She held my head I immediately calmed down and saw a warm golden light fill my closed eyes and ripple through my body in waves of sweet Mother love. When I first gazed into Her eyes I experienced them as dancing playfully in mine. The following days and nights were full of joy and wonder. My dreaming was more vivid, colorful and profound than ever before. Each Darshan varied greatly. I entered timelessness and melted into the vastness of Her Being. The last evening I felt an extraordinary fluttering in my third eye. I remained aware of this odd and exciting sensation for several days.

I have made the journey to Thalheim a number of times since my first encounter with Mother and each time I return home more deeply connected to the Divine in the challenges and opportunities that unfold daily. There has been some physical discomfort. Mostly a fairly intense pressure in my forehead from time to time. But of course there is discomfort when one's entire architecture is being reshaped as I have felt mine has been since Her hands first held my head.

Last visit James Broughton and I stayed in Mother's home. What an honor to be so close to Her. Being able to see Her in the garden looking up to smile is an image forever etched in my memory. I am an artist and now I find myself most fulfilled when making images of Her. To disseminate images of Her is becoming a glorious obsession. I was recently able to say in words to Her what I had previously said only in silence. I love you Mother.

35.

Mother Meera, the Mother Energy

To love and worship the sublime is a force that seeks fulfilment in each and everyone of us. This force expresses itself in various ways. Some see the sublime through the trusting eyes of a child. Others hear the sublime through a voice or a violin. Still others feel the sublime through an adoration for the truth.

Each person's concept of truth can be their own, but for me, truth is not spoken, but felt. I feel it each time I am uplifted. The intensity of these moments of truth vary from ecstasy, clarity and revelation, to pathos, compassion and even pain. There is a restlessness in me, that drives me to feel these moments of truth with ever growing intensity. In other words, I feel truth often through tears, or through the sharing of beauty, where the warmth of love and joy is present. I associate truth more with feeling the truth, rather than with thinking or speaking the truth.

Feeling joy, rapture and wonder while listening to music, is quite different from knowing about the technical skill required to perform that music. We all have access to the exalted experience, even if we don't participate in the rigid discipline required to play the violin to perfection. This ability to feel sublime moments creates a communication bond among the listeners, as through listening, they have the possibility to touch the sublime in each other.

The same communication bond can take place through reading a book, an article or a poem. Something electric occured within me when I read the book *Answers* by Mother Meera. It was as if all my moments of sublime exaltation through music, poetry, philosophy and prayer were culminating into a crescendo. It was as if the entire cosmos of opposite forces was merging into unity, clarity, simplicity and truth. I now read the book daily, and use its contents literally. I was amazed at the results, but am not amazed any more. Divine alchemy works like a clock, just like digestion and assimilation works in the physical body. Food through digestion and assimilation is transformed, so that it can be absorbed by the blood to nourish us. In the same way, I find that when I digest and assimilate the words of Mother Meera, they transform the chemistry of my feelings, so that I am better able to dwell in the realm of peace rather than conflict.

During Easter, we were at our mountain cabin, and one evening my son and I were having a relaxed conversation after my husband and all the other children had gone to bed. They were all tired after a long day of skiing. My son and daughter-in-law, after six years of marriage had no child. It had become a sensitive subject and I felt that it was difficult to discuss, without triggering hurt feelings. However, that evening, my son brought up the subject and said that he and his wife were quite resigned to not having a child. He reiterated that they were lucky in so many other ways, and if no soul wished to come to them, they would build a good life even if they could not have a child.

I felt disconsolate and powerless to say anything, so when I finally went to bed, I took the book *Answers*, held it close to my heart then lifted

Mr. Reddy   Mother Meera   Adolakshmi   India 1979

it and opened it. It opened on page 101, the chapter on prayer. The question was, "What should I ask you for"? Mother Meera answers: *"Ask for everything, like a child asks its mother for eveything, without shame. Do not stop at peace of mind or purity of heart or surrender. Demand everything. Don't be satisfied with anything less than everything. If you ask, you will receive. If you receive, you will have to bear."*

I went to sleep with this answer and was at peace, because I knew that I was going to ask Mother Meera to help my children. I had not yet met Mother Meera, but I decided that I would write a letter. The next day I drafted a letter, long, emotional and overwrought. After reading through it, I felt that I would really be trying the patience of an angel if such a wordy epistle appeared in all its melodramatic nuances. My common sense made me write on a card, so that I had to squeeze the contents on two small pages. I was short and concise, yet I felt that every word carried my faith and trust. I just knew that the Mother would help.

After I had posted the letter to the Mother and enclosed a photo of my son and daughter-in-law, I felt that the matter was no longer in my hands. I somehow did not need confirmation as I felt an inner peace. Almost a month later I phoned Mother Meera's home to make an appointment for my husband and myself to come to darshan. Adilakshmi said: "The Mother has received your letter, Anil Horn, and says that your daughter-in-law will conceive, but both of them must ask for help themselves." I was overwhelmed and asked, "Should they say the mantra, Om Namo Bhagavate Mata Meera?" "No", replied Adilakshmi, "That is not necessary. It is sufficient to say, 'Mother Meera, help us'."

After this telephone conversation I was happy and quietly content. I phoned my son and asked him if I could visit them the following day as it was his birthday. I arrived there with a small photo of Mother Meera and with a copy of the book *Answers*. I told them about my conversation on the phone and I gave them the photo saying: "Light incense before the Mother and ask for help, and you will have a child as the Mother has blessed you."

They both looked enthusiastic and my daughter-in-law said that she would frame the photo, and they would both request the Mother to bless them with a child. I don't think it will surprise anybody to hear that a month later my son informed me that his wife had conceived.

The eternal wisdom of the Mother struck me. Her help was forthcoming, but the participation of my son and daughter-in-law became necessary, if they wanted to be blessed with a child. My request was not enough. Even though my faith for the Mother was instrumental in formulating the request, yet I was not allowed to intefere in their life, even though I knew that they wanted a child. They themselves had to make the effort of asking. As they responded to the Mother's picture, I felt that the protection of the Mother was surrounding them already.

I continued to ask the Mother for everything, just like a child. For myself, I asked for the purity of heart to daily pray and meditate with devotion and humility. This is because I had earlier come across my own spiritual pride that had often blinded me from feeling the truth. Mentally I knew so much, but my knowledge had blinded my heart. I could give every conceivable explanation and solution for every problem, but what use was that, if I could not solve my own problems.

My answer came on page 96 where the Mother speaks about spiritual experiences. *"If there is pride or vanity, then you are not awake. The really great saints and yogis are always the most humble. Humility is love, humility is what the heart knows. True joy is humble because it is pure and given. A humble man is always quick to see his mistakes. Unless you are humble, the Divine will not use you. My power will only pass through you when you are clear, otherwise it would be dangerous for you. You must keep yourself clear at all times. The ego will keep on trying to seize for itself what the soul is learning."*

These words gave me a chance to recognize how I had earlier misinterpreted divine grace by turning it into spiritual superiority. This superiority had prevented me from progressing on the spiritual path. I had often felt the Divine so close, but the loss of that feeling came when I approached others through my mental capacity and not through my feeling heart. The need to replenish my heart again and again with love, devotion, sacrifice and surrender became imperative if I was to feel and experience the Divine constantly.

As long as words like "God" and "the Divine Mother" are comprehended mentally, they are a concept to be analyzed. Intellectual pride will very soon discard them as fantasy or a crutch for the weak to lean on. We seldom through our mental pride accept that even if we dismiss these concepts, we might very well develop the tendency to lean on other crutches. This is not because we want to lean on crutches, but our environment feeds us on information that makes us dependent on temporary happiness. We are almost brain washed into believing that the crutches of temporary joy can give us permanent happiness.

The human feeling heart is capable of tremendous depths of feeling, but when it is deprived of the stimulation it craves, it begins to rely on the passing whims of pleasure. These are the crutches through which independence and freedom disappear, as we lose the capacity to call upon our inner resources when faced with conflict. It is impossible to cooperate harmoniously with others, unless we build the resources within to experience the highest and best in each other.

For me, Mother Meera is the way that is helping me to make the quantum leap into the light, where I am able to unite with the radiance that is more divine than human. Living close to the Mother in heart and soul purifies my own thoughts, feelings and motives, as I can almost feel an unbelievable clarity dawning in my understanding. I seemed to have been stuck for years in a groove, as if I was moving back and forth horizontally, and the monotony of this groove was imprisoning me into a mundane thought and feeling pattern. Now I feel that the Mother is the mover and I am the doer.

On page 39, the following question is put to Mother Meera. "What is the most profound experience for you?" The Mother answers: *"When people are happy, that is the most profound experience for me."*

This might sound simple and easy to some, but being happy is an evolved state through which a realized person transcends inherent tension making traumas. My heart tells me that I can trust the Mother to enlighten me, mainly because I trust the sincerity of the Mother to put me into harmony with that which is close to the Divine. In other words I would much rather be peaceful, joyful, harmonious and happy, rather than mean, selfish, miserable and hostile. If I work to maintain this inner peace and joy, I feel I am in affinity with the Mother and with all those who are in a state of bliss and happiness within themselves.

On page 108 Mother Meera says: *"If you are fixed on my outer personality and outer form, conflict and disappointment can arise. But if your inner relatioship to me is good, then all is well."*

This inner relationship with the Mother is exceedingly important to me. It is my barometer through which I maintain my inner strength, joy and peace. It is the guardian within me, that steers me into acting with compassion and dignity in most situations. At times I have experienced that impossible conflicts arise in daily life when others get nasty for no rhyme or reason. At that moment it is extremely tempting to shout, argue, accuse and fight. But ever since I met Mother Meera, I don't want to do that, as the inner contact with the Mother would weaken if I leaped to my defence by throwing recriminations at those who try to hurt me. Through my love for the Divine in the Mother, I will not jeopardize that love, as it is the guardian that puts me into affinity with the Divine. It is very cold and lonely to be alienated from this love. Walking hand in hand with the Divine has become an integral part of my well-being, through which I am able to maintain a constant state of affinity with the Mother.

I am reminded of a little story about walking hand in hand with God which I would like to relate. A devoted disciple of God, named Lal once met a thief on the corner of a road. The thief, in one swift move, grabbed the purse of Lal, who got furious and started swearing and hitting the thief in a rage. The thief had been ready to run away with the purse, but when Lal lost his temper, the thief got inflamed and started beating Lal in blind fury. Poor Lal was left by the roadside, bruised, bleeding, and unconscious. When he finally awoke, Lal looked up, and could feel the hand of God lifting him up. Lal accusingly asked, "Where were you, God? Is this the way to treat your disciple, leaving him to be beaten by a savage thief?"

God chuckled and said good humouredly, "I was right beside you, protecting you, until you got into a rage and forgot me. When you started to swear and fight, I became superfluous. So I moved away and went to help those who called upon my name. But come along now. Here is your purse. While the thief stumbled, your purse fell on the ground. I will now attend to your wounds, and you will soon be healed." God smiled indulgently while Lal sulked, limping along, but still walking hand in hand with God!

The chemistry of divine intervention is difficult to understand. All that we can say is, "that it happens". Some will explain it away as coincidence, whereas others just know through the rhythm of their heartbeat when help comes from above, and when it is coincidence.

My daughters visited Mexico and the United States during their summer holidays. They travel on standby tickets, as their father is a pilot. The planes were all heavily booked, so before their departure I had said, "If you are stuck, just ask Mother Meera for help." The plane from Frankfurt to Mexico was overbooked. They waited at the gate, and their chances didn't look too promising. Eventually they got the last two seats. They put it down to coincidence. I had, however, with full sincerety prayed and asked the Mother to help them, so my gut feeling was that even on a fully booked flight they would get on.

After staying a month in Mexico, they decided to fly to Seattle, via Houston, and discovered that during that very week all the flights from Houston to Seattle were fully booked due to a Seafair. But, they had to chance it, as their grand-aunt was expecting them in Seattle that very week. At the Houston airport, they saw flight after flight take off, and then one of them formulated the worlds, "Mother Meera help us." They got on the next flight. Coincidence?

After spending ten days in Seattle they were due to return home. They were told that their chances were good from New York to Scandinavia, so off they flew to New York. Upon arrival, they were informed that every flight had got booked on that day and the next three days. They stood at the airport, once again watching flight after flight take off. Then my younger daughter said to her sister, "If Mother Meera gets us on a flight today, I will go and visit the Mother." Within the next half hour they were on a flight to Europe!

There can be many interpretations to this sort of incident, and in a way, it might not be the best way to recommend the Mother to others. One of my sons once remarked, "Mama, you can't treat the Divine like a supermarket where you say, 'You deliver, and I'll pay'!"

In actual fact, this is exactly what we should be able to understand in our world of supersonic communication. Thought is the instant link with the divine world – a sort of instant cordless telephone! It is not necessary that Mother Meera herself is waiting at the other end to pick up the phone at that very moment. But surely, there is a subtle and instantaneous communication between the divine world, and help comes when the call is sincere.

The concept of the Divine Mother is primordial, and through this energy, the children of the earth have always received the impulse to love more, so that we can protect and cherish the creation that is put in our care. Through the last few centuries there has been a distancing from this Mother energy, as the human heart has lost touch with its inner core. Discovering the Divine Mother is not a new fad or another trend. We human beings only recapture what exists in out primordial memory. The Divine Mother has always existed. If we fail to recognise this within our hearts, it does not nullify this power. The time is coming for the human heart to melt, as the heart has been under great pressure. It has been restricted to force itself into listening to analytical limitations that has put it in a capsule of miniscule capacity.

On page 45 Mother Meera is asked if it really is the Virgin Mary who is appearing at Medjugorje. Mother Meera answers: *"Yes, she is appearing in Medjugorje. Because people find it difficult to believe that an embodied form could really be Jesus and Mary, they are coming as appearances such as that at Medjugorje. Mary has the quelity of motherhood. She is appearing to protect her children. She expresses compassion."*

The story of overcoming evil with good is also imprinted in human primordial memory. That is why children can understand the tales of Hans Christian Anderson with their heart. There is a haunting beauty in evil, as deep down the heart knows that human courage has the power to conquer evil and transform it. A child can easily and naturally accept the power of the Divine Mother. What could be more natural for a child?

I have always prayed to the Blessed Virgin even though I am not a Catholic. I have not tried to make my daughters or sons pray to Our Lady, but somewhere in their awareness, they have felt my faith. I did not know that, until they brought the pictures to me of Our Lady of Guadalupe from Mexico. Perhaps that is why they can with an open heart visit Mother Meera, as she is in physical form embodying the same energy of the Divine Mother.

When compassion and love pours out from any mother, she expresses the sweet emanations of the Divine Mother, and is in affinity with the holy practice of compassionate giving. For three years I had prayed to the Virgin Mary to bless my son and daughter-in-law with a child. Eventually, when Mother Meera blessed them with a child, it was easy for me to see that my prayers to Our Lady had been answered through Mother Meera. For me, Mother Meera represents the same energy, the same light and the same compassion as the Blessed Mother Mary.

The children of the earth are craving for this compasionate love. What the heart seeks, the heart gets. I have faith that many will receive solace and peace through the blessings of the Mother, just as I have.

Mother Meera, the transforming power.

While staying at one of the hotels in the vicinity of Thalheim, the breakfast table, after the previous nights darshan often gets to be the meeting place of those who have come to see Mother Meera from all over the world. They automatically flock together, and the conversation invariably revolves around their experiences which range from curiosity, excitement, faith and doubt to understanding, devotion and mystical ecstasy. All these emotions or opinions are part of the transformative process from the old self to the divine self.

Each of us reacts or responds according to the inbuilt structure of our consciousness. Some might come with expectations of transformation through a burst of light, whereas others might start relating their spiritual revelations and experiences. No matter how scattered or intense the views become, it might be a good idea to just look at the situation through the Mother's own words.

When asked on page 12, "What is your main purpose", the Mother answers. *"It is to help humans and to make them happy, peaceful, contented, harmonious and loving. Happiness and spiritual growth are connected. Being peaceful and being happy form the most important foundation of spiritual practise. Then the practise goes by itself."*

Being peaceful and being happy is a fundamental desire of every human being, but it is an art that needs to be learned and practised. What begins as an art eventually turns into a science, when we gradually begin to master the contents of Mother Meera's *Answers*.

Science affirms that a hyothesis is proved when an experiment is repeated and identical results occur. To be peaceful and happy, we need to make certain internal experiments through which we discover what gives us peace and happiness. The wonderful thing about the Mother is that we are given total freedom. There are no rigid set of rules, no penances or disciplines that have to be adhered to in a slavish manner.

All the answers of the Mother are simple yet profound. They are an entire philosophy, yet easy to comprehend. Even if we are able to absorb everything rapidly, we will only put into practise that which concerns us in the immediate present. Having earlier read volumes upon volumes of scripture and philosophy, I have seldom come across a work that can in so few words be instrumental in a total transformative process of the human being.

Of course the power of the book *Answers*, lies in the spirit of the Mother, whose words are an inspiring and vibrating force that gives energy to the disciple. The Mother's power penetrates us, when our aspiration to love and learn is sincere.

Prayer, meditation, good conduct, kindness, love and compassion are the standard methods through which the old self grows into the divine self. So what is new about this book, *Answers*? It is Mother Meera herself. A disciple asks on page 40, "The Mother has many faces, withdrawn, majestic, mischievous, angry, tender. Which is the real face?" Mother Meera answers: "*All are real, but the most real face is the face of love. Keep gazing on that, whatever happens. Turn to that in whatever difficulties you experience. Revere that through whatever pain you are passing, and you will be given every joy and every courage. Perfect love of the Mother is to see her face of love in everything that happens. If you attain that love you will be able to do anything. There is a Telugu song. 'Love can melt the stone, turn the mountain to water.' Perfect love can never be defeated because it is infinite.*"

Each person will experience the Mother according to their own needs, their own emotions or their own mental concepts. But one thing is universal about the Divine Mother, and that is that the love of the Divine Mother is boundless and always has been.

The Divine Mother cannot resist love from any child. A deep and abiding love binds the Divine Mother to her children when their devotion is sincere and pure. Devotion makes it possible for the Divine Mother to reside in the heart of a disciple at all times. When the Divine Mother resides within the heart, the error margin decreases, and an increased sensitivity to danger can intuitively avert accidents and calamities.

Love is something that everyone understands, yet love has a strange quality. It cannot be forced, and it cannot be mentally cultivated. I cannot to tell you to love the Divine Mother, unless something within you moves you to feel adoration, devotion and respect. Even you yourself cannot will yourself to love the Divine Mother, unless you are warned by the sweetness that emanates from the Mother.

Thalheim, Germany 1984

Culturally our civilization has lost the significance of maintaining a contact with the Divine Mother. The idea of God, or the Heavenly Father is better imprinted on the information field of most people. This concept has been kept alive by the religions who visualize God as a masculine monotheistic power. Mother Meera refers to God as Paramatman.

On page 18, Mother Meera describes Paramatman: *"Paramatman is infinite light and the source of all, of being, knowledge, bliss, of peace, of each atman, each soul."*

Asked if there is a difference between Paramatman and his light, Mother Meera answers: *"In a way Paramatman is in everything in all creation – earth, water, fire, air, sky, animals – at all times. But we can see the light only sometimes. The light has the quality of love, grace, power, bliss, jnana. Without it, nothing can exist."* It becomes more and more clear for us that enlightenment comes through the light, which in a human being takes on the radiance of love, grace, power, bliss, and wisdom.

I, who have been to darshan and pranam, know that the feelings vary with each darshan. But one thing I am aware of, and that is that I feel a process is set in motion within me, the effects of which will continue all through my life. These effects move the inner core of my personality, or even shake it. Clarity, compassion, aspiration, and devotion are the heights that are experienced, but at the same time, my human defects are churned up in an uncomfortable way. With humility, I am almost forced to face the not too nice sides of my nature, that with dogged persistence often push me into having an ego trip.

This ego at times fills me with feelings of self righteousness and self pity through which I easily find myself blaming others. It also pushes me into defending and justifying myself by feeling superior. In other words, the ego is everywhere, in me and around me, speaking and acting through me in a subtle, yet quite obnoxious way. The ego is so devious, that at times it even manages to convince me that the other person has an overpowering ego, exactly when my own ego is playing its own trump card to get control!

These ego games have gone on for years, but since I met the Mother, I seem to have received the blessings of divine grace, that enable me to laugh when I play games with my ego. These games of hide and seek are great fun, because instead of attacking and blaming others, I get hold of my ego and every time I catch it, I win. But if it catches me, I lose that game.

On page 115, a disciple puts the following question to Mother Meera: "Must the dismantling of the ego always feel like a death?" The Mother answers: *"To achieve realization a dying of the old self, the ego, is necessary. But why be sad about it? What has the old self given you that you should love it so? The divine self will give you all things and also give you bliss. Do not think in terms of giving up anything. Think of growing. Think of always growing stronger and more loving and more complete. Then what you wanted yesterday, you will not want today and what you wanted today, tomorrow you will see is not useful. Discipline must be there, and control – not in the name of death, but in the name of love and true life. You have to cut a tree sometimes to make it straight and help it grow."*

When the old self is transformed by the divine it enters into a new birth, through which the divine self takes birth. In this growth and shaping of the divine self, the Divine Mother for me is playing a formative role, through which my progress is accelerated and my will is strengthened. By putting myself in the Mother's care and protection, I feel that I am able to maintain a constant inner contact with the Mother, that grows with each day.

Having lived for more than half a century, and since adolescence having intellectually enjoyed reading the great philosophers, the simple fact dawned on me, that if this knowledge is to be of any use to me, I must experience it working within me as a living vibrating peace. I know of so many people who have gone to their grave, sad and unfulfilled, as they were unable to transform their knowledge into harmonious living. Why should I be stupid and make the same mistake? Far better to radiate warmth and happiness than to spread misery all around!

Put in another way, I could say that the divine qualities are a latent power within me, but for a latent energy to manifest an electric current is necessary. As this current is sometimes missing, I plug in to the Mother, and immediately the light goes on. I feel charged as the electrical current starts circulating and I am able to enchance my own light. When I switch off, my consciousness, like a computer, stores the light and wisdom of the Mother. When I switch on again, I am able to connect up and my consciousness gets recharged with more power throught the radiating energy of the Mother.

I think people are becoming more and more aware that children receive damaging or constructive information through the emanations of their parents' feelings. This information can very well be responsible for their formative process that breeds philanthrophists or egoists. Through my contact with the Mother, I am aware that the process of spiritual alchemy within me has been speeded up. I am able to size up situations in a matter of seconds, so I don't blunder into making foolish moves that can damage or destroy relationships. It requires skill to make love work, and that, I think, is my most urgent need in this incarnation. Through the Mother, I am able to clear the dedbris that has piled up through past tensions and past karmic accumulations.

When talking about spiritual experiences on page 98, the Mother says: *"Remember that however extraordinary the experiences, there are always further and greater experiences. The mind is finite, but the spirit is infinite. There is no limit to transformation. The transformation I am doing is within the being and power of God and so limitless by nature."*

I do not believe that I have to die before I experience the miracle of light. I know that for me this is possible in this body and in this life. I know in the deepest recesses of my soul that the destiny of a human being is far far grander than we have been lead to believe. I also know that this grand destiny is not mapped out for a few selected souls. It is the heritage of the entire human race, and the transformative process is definitely being speeded up by the sublime holiness that is poured out through the sweet presence of Mother Meera upon this earth.

Mother Meera, the benevolent avatar

When I was in India in January, my sister and I decided to drive to Jaipur for a few days. As we drove by the Amer fort in the evening, it was beautifully lit up and looked hauntingly majestic. We realized that it was lit up because it was the 26th of January, which is India's republic day. We mentioned this to out hosts when we arrived in Jaipur and they suggested that we should return to the fort for the aarti in the evening. After a cup of tea, we all piled into the car and drove to the fort. It looked even more magnificent now as the full moon was resplendently shining on it, making it look like a charmed castle where the gods and goddesses dwell in blissful joy.

When we arrived at the temple of the Mother Kali, we saw that people were coming out of the temple and were disappointed, as we thought we had come too late for the aarti. However, when we went into the temple we were told that another aarti would take place at 8 p.m. We were quite content to wait, so we sat on the cold marble benches and happily chatted away. Half an hour later the temple bell rang. We jumped up and went into the temple. We realized that there were no other people but us. It was as if the Mother was giving us a special audience.

The aarti is the evening ritual prayer when candles are lit on a tray and the tray is moved in a rhythmic circular movement in front of the picture or statue of the deity. The temple that evening was saturated with power, and the atmosphere was charged with energy. The curtain in front of the statue of the Mother Kali was drawn back. While the aarti was being performed I prayed with my hands joined, asking the Mother to let me know and feel the power of light in my mind and heart. I also prayed that I should become closer to the Divine Mother in this incarnation.

Mother Meera, the loving parent

Some of us, as we grow up find that our relationship with our mother or father has been difficult or complicated. We suffer, because we don't know how to analyze the problems. Our loyalty and respect for our parents stop us from being honest about our traumas. Facing facts sometimes leads to disillusionment, so we avoid calling a spade a spade, as by doing that some of our childhood dreams would be shattered.

Ever since I met Mother Meera, I have stopped crying or complaining about all the relationships that did not turn out as expected. Whenever I feel deprived of love or understanding, I turn to the Divine Mother. When I am sad and lonely, I speak through my thought to the Mother. I tell her about my anguish, just as I would tell a loving parent. Every time I have done this, I have within hours felt as if I am enfolded by the protection of an understanding parent. I have felt waves of unconditional love moving into me, where no demands, no criticism, and no judgement are made. I feel loved and cared for as I am, naked in all my imperfections.

Once when I felt these waves of love flowing through me, I wept and wept, and I took the Mother's book *Answers* and held it close to my breast. Gradually, as my sobs became exhausted, I opened the book at random and found myself reading the chapter on Love and Devotion on page 105. The Mother says: *"Mr. Reddy used to say often how strange it was that men would weep for the loss of money or a woman, but not spend one sleepless night praying for God. Ramakrishna used to say that also. Look how much he wept and prayed for the Divine Mother. It is a great thing to weep for God. How often do people weep for a lover who then throws them away! But God remembers every small prayer, every tear. A tear is a door through which I can come. How can I come into a heart that doesn't long for me."*

When I read this, I just knew that my tears of longing had been the door through which the Mother had sent me these waves of love and protection. At that moment the Divine Mother became my mother and father as I felt a parent's protective love flowing towards me to console me.

My husband is not "spiritually inclined" according to the traditional meaning of this term. He is a man of action, but I think that his deeds are spiritual, as through them he is constantly helping those around him. Even though he is extremely active, there is a quiet place in his consciousness that is able to perceive the spiritual power of the Mother. Once when I was sad and weary, he saw that I had been crying. He looked at me with tenderness and wiping away my tears, he said, "Don't weep, think of Mother Meera instead, and you will be happy."

One day I was deeply concerned about a complicated problem in which many of my relations were involved. I did not know how to ask for help, as just explaining the entire problem to the Mother would have taken pages. It almost would have required giving the family's history as wheels within wheels were churning. I thought it would be better to phone Adilakshmi and ask her to request the Mother to bless and help everyone who was involved. When I phoned, the telephone was engaged. That to me is usually a sign that I need to wait. The disturbed feeling within me confirmed that I must be quiet and not rush into talking. So I left the phone and went into the kitchen.

On the previous day, my husband and I had picked up buckets full of blueberries in the forest, so I started to prepare them for freezing. While picking out the leaves, I became still and totally at peace, and the disturbed feeling was suddenly gone. In these moments, I can almost feel the presence of an angel, as the contrast from disturbance to peace is very marked. In a flash I knew exactly how I was going to help my family with their current problem. I saw which course of action I should take, whom I should contact, and how they could resolve their differences. It was as if once again the inner telephone link with the

Mother had been opened. Through that I was able to get my answers clearly and concisely. Once again the Mother had shown herself as the wise and benevolent parent, as within minutes, I had a definite course of action to follow.

That day, I thought very much about karma. We all have karmic links with our family, because their joys and sorrows have an effect upon us, as we become sad when they suffer and are happy when they are happy. Karma is the law of cause and effect, or put more simply, we reap what we sow. Even if we sometimes think that we are being burdened by suffering and bad fortune, and there might appear an injustice in the pain we have to bear, we are forced to accept our fate. This is because past deeds, past thoughts, past feelings, in this life or previous lives, all move through a cleansing process. Through this process we have a chance to clear the debris of our mean and nasty deeds and move on. Karma is not punishment, but opportunity, through which we can change and transform ourselves.

When I surrender to the Mother, I surrender to the beauty, sweetness and unfathomable wisdom of a loving and all knowing parent. On page 127, the question is, "What is a realized man like?" The Mother answers: *"Like a child at peace in the womb of the Mother, knowing he is sustained at every moment by the grace and light of the Divine mother."*

That is how I would like to live, sustained by the grace and light of the Divine Mother and protected by the Heavenly Father. I see both these parents before my eyes when I behold the tender love of Mother Meera, which I cherish with my whole heart.

MOTHER MEERA

An attempt to describe the Indescribable

The body of Mother Meera is transformation
The existence of Mother Meera is peace
The steps of Mother Meera are humility
The action of Mother Meera is compassion
The effect of Mother Meera is virtue
The voice of Mother Meera is OM
The tongue of Mother Meera is silence
The teaching of Mother Meera is freedom
The knowledge of Mother Meera is wisdom
The hearing of Mother Meera is the fulfillment of our
desires
The thinking of Mother Meera is the only religion
The feeling of Mother Meera is a limitless flowing out of
Herself
The sight of Mother Meera is rebirth
The touch of Mother Meera is the dream of gentleness
The love of Mother Meera is yoga
The presence of Mother Meera is samadhi
The grace of Mother Meera is desirelessness
The life of Mother Meera is permanent sacrifice
The being of Mother Meera is truth
The home of Mother Meera is the heart of all beings

August 19, 1987
A Devotee

She comes
In the pure exchange...
The Trees hold Her voice
a moment
Purple cheek
Smile of silver

Snow

I awake
Under the freshness of Her foot
On my neck

And celebrate the night
With all the strings of Her heart

A Devotee

MOTHER MEERA

... physical incarnation of the Divine Consciousness on
earth.

We know that God is Love.
In Mother Meera we meet with Love in a person.
The hands of Love touch us,
Love's eyes speak a tender welcome.

Heaven receives us when we look into these eyes.
It opens towards us like a rose-garden,
embraces us,
takes us into its heart.

In the Divine Heart we are born anew.
In the heart of the Divine Presence every burden
is relieved, every longing stilled.

Our soul rejoices.
We have come home.

It is the return of the soul into the Light.

A Devotee

Mr. Reddy is with two Mothers blessing and giving Light to Him. At the same time, the Light is coming to the earth. The two trees are the first to respond to it.
August 8, 1987

EPILOGUE

Mother does not want to form a cult. She does not want to establish a series of ashrams. She has no interest whatsoever in being the center of any kind of religion. Her work is for no small band of initiates, no special selected cadre of "highly developed" souls, but for the whole world. Any vanity of election on the part of Her devotees She dislikes and will prevent at the first opportunity – any sense of being spiritually special, any sense at all that prevents us from doing Her Work which is to open to the Light She is calling down into existence, and to surrender with all our hearts and minds and souls to the Divine. Her demand is perfect in its simplicity and Her Work will be done with or without devotees. It is not the Mother who has any need of us; it is we who need Her.

Mother says, "IF YOU CAN, PRAY TO THE SUPREME DIRECTLY." She urges everyone to address Paramatman without intermediaries. "THAT IS THE BEST WAY. IF YOU NEED AN INTERMEDIARY, PRAY TO HIM THROUGH AN INCARNATION." Mother claims no precedence; "ALL INCARNATIONS ARE EQUAL." They appear different because they have different tasks to do in world history but really they are one. Mother is in all Divine Forms and all Divine Forms are in Her. Many of Her devotees have seen Her as Durga, Kali, Lakshmi, as Krishna and Sri Aurobindo, and as the Virgin. Mother wants no one to change their religion; She is not interested in "conversion". For Her it has no meaning. Whatever Incarnation you believe in, pray to Him or Her with all your heart and soul. All prayers sincerely addressed to the Divine go to Her; all sincere cries of the soul are heard and answered by Her; all pure openings to the Divine are openings to Her and Her Light. Mother's work is for the world, for all creeds, for all castes and all colours. She is the Mother of us all and in Her Love we should live in peace and love.

Let the Transformation of the earth be accomplished.
Let Her Work be done.

MOTHER

An eaglet comes out of the nest,
Looks here and there and everywhere
For Mother, who is nowhere.
She made up her mind to take no rest
Until she finds her loving Mother.

Soaring in the brilliant sky
She asked the radiant sun
If he has seen her sweet Mother.
Upon hearing her bitter cry
Woefully he says, "She isn't here."

Swooping down to the emerald earth
She asks the glittering golden sea,
"Have you seen my compassionate Mother?"
With her deep long breath
"No," sorrowfully replies she.

From morning time till evening
She is mourning for her dear Mother.
Looking at the twinkling stars
And silver shining moon, she hurries
Home with heavy broken heart.

Rolling down tears like pearls
Of a broken string, she sobs
Bitterly, "Mother, darling Mother,
Benevolent Mother! Show me
Thy marvellous face! Without
Thee I am not. Come, come
Soon and embrace me."

In stillness she hears a voice
She looks to the right and to the
Left and up and down
Without finding a single soul.
She wonders whence the sound
Comes.

Suddenly she looks within
In her golden chamber she sees
The Mighty Mother throned.
Her brilliant face gives the Light.
Her radiant smile heals suffering.
Her wide shining eyes assure delight.

Her beauty gives ecstasy,
Her presence blows away the darkness,
And spreads the light everywhere.
Giving up myself to the lotus feet
In silence humbly and dumbly
I am merged in Her Supreme Love.

Adilakshmi

NAMES AND TERMS

Sri Aurobindo: The greatest Indian yogi and philosopher of modern times. He lived most of his yogic life in Pondicherry, in French India. He was the author of several metaphysical masterpieces, the greatest of which is *The Life Divine*. He was also a great poet and wrote an epic poem, *Savitri*. The yoga of Sri Aurobindo which is indebted to traditional Indian yogas, transcends their limitations. It is an Integral Yoga, a yoga that does not deny or flee life as illusion, but desires the complete and radical transformation of life on earth. Sri Aurobindo's task was to call down into the consciousness of the earth the Supramental Light, that would enable the transformation of life into the Divine Life, and to make humanity aware of that Light and open to it.

Sweet Mother: Sri Aurobindo's Shakti or Divine Partner in the work of transformation. A French woman, She lived in Pondicherry and began the Ashram there. She is worshipped as an Incarnation of Divine Mother by Her devotees. It was Sweet Mother's task to bring down the Supramental Light into the consciousness of the earth and She did so in 1956, thus making the transformation certain. She left the body in 1973 at the age of ninety-five.

Adishakti: The original Shakti. The Supreme Mother.

AUM: The Absolute. Another spelling of "OM".

Avadhuta: A realized soul. A person identified with the Supreme.

Brahma: The Creator.

Bull: A vehicle of God Shiva.

Chariot: A vehicle of Lord Krishna.

Cow: A symbol of light or consciousness or power of purification. The white light or spiritual consciousness.

Darshan: Self-revelation of the deity to the devotee.

Devaloka: The world of Gods and Goddesses.

Durga: The conquering and protecting aspects of the Universal Mother.

Elephant: The vehicle of Goddess Lakshmi. Also a symbol of strength illumined by wisdom; or of the power to remove obstacles.

Ganapati: The power that removes obstacles by the force of Knowledge.

Gods and Goddesses: The personalities or powers put forth by the Divine.

Ishwara: The Lord. Also a name for Shiva.

Kali: The Mother of Force and Strength.

Karthikeya: God of Victory.

Lakshmi: Goddess of Supreme Love and Delight.

Lion: Indicates force, courage, strength, and power.

Loka: World.

Lotus: The symbol of Divine Presence.

Maha: Great.

Maheshwari: Goddess of supreme Knowledge.

Milk: Symbol of the flow of the higher consciousness.

Nagendra: King of serpents. The serpent is a symbol of force or energy.

Nirguna Parabrahman: Pure Consciousness without attributes.

Nirvana: The liberated condition of the being.   \

Overmind: Plane of consciousness beyond the individual and universal mind.

Paramatman: The Supreme Self, the Absolute, the Supreme Divine Being.

Parvati: Spouse of Shiva.

Puja: Ceremony of gratitude to the master or to a deity.

Rama: A divine incarnation.

Rishi: A seer.

Sadhana: Spiritual practice and self-discipline.

Samadhi: A sacred tomb for the preservation of a holy body after death.

Saraswati: Goddess of Learning and Perfection.

Shakti: Energy and power.

Shaktipat: Transmission of spiritual power (shakti) from guru to disciple; spiritual awakening by grace.

Siddhi: The fruit of sadhana.

Shiva: Another name for Ishwara.

Supramental: The plane of consciousness above the Overmind.

Tapasya: Practice of Yoga.

Tiger: Vehicle of Durga.

Trisul: A trident. The weapon of Gods and Goddesses.

Vishnu: The Protector, the Lord of Protection.

Yamaloka: The world where the God of Death lives.

Yamaraj: The God of Death.

Yoga: Union with the Divine.

Montréal, Canada 1979

Darshan Information

Mother Meera gives Darshan each Friday, Saturday, Sunday, and Monday. It begins at 7 o'clock in the evening. People should be at the Townhall (Mehrzweckhalle) of Thalheim by 18:30 CET. As space is limited, people are requested to call and make a reservation some weeks in advance. Reservations can be made only by phone between 10 a.m. and 4 p.m. seven days a week. All correspondence to Mother should be made in: Telugu (Mother's mother tongue), English, or German.

Mother Meera's permanent address is:

Oberdorf 4a
65599 Dornburg-Thalheim
Germany
Phone +49-(0)6436-2305
Fax +49-(0)6436-2361
Compu Serve 100342,2574

The following books about Mother Meera are available at the above address:

Answers by Mother Meera in English, German and French
The Mother by Adilakshmi in English, German and French
Bringing Down the Light – Paintings by Mother Meera

Photos of Mother Meera are available in 3 sizes
10x15 cm, 15x20 cm, and 20x30 cm

Directions to Mother Meera's Home

Dornburg is a group of 5 villages 15 km north of the town of Limburg which is situated between Frankfurt and Cologne (Köln). After you have made your darshan reservations by phone, please make your own hotel booking. Come dressed normally and with washed hair and arrive at the car park at the «Mehr-zweck-halle» (Town hall, Salle Polyvalente) in Thalheim at 18.30 (6:30 p.m.). This is the meeting point for all visitors. Do not park anywhere else. There is no advantage to come earlier. Do not go to the houses in the villages and ask for rooms or information. Children are not allowed to come; they will get Mother's blessings through their parents. Elder people should be able to sit quiet for three hours. Mother gives answers through the secretary by phone from 16.00 to 17.00 hrs (4 p.m. to 5 p.m.) on Fri, Sat, Sun & Mon.

Travelling by train from Frankfurt airport: Tickets to Limburg, Hadamar, Dornburg-Frickhofen, Wilsenroth and Willmenrod can be purchased at the "Travel center" below the airport Terminal 1 B. 1) Shuttle train: airport – Frankfurt central station 2) Frankfurt – Limburg: some direct trains or with an easy change across the platform at Niedernhausen 3) Local train: Limburg – your destination.

Travelling by train from other directions:
Via Koblenz (west) - Limburg or via Gießen/Wetzlar (east) - Limburg

Bus Nr. 4280 departs opposite Limburg train station (near church) via Hadamar-Niederzeuzheim-Dornburg villages. During the week the bus leaves Limburg about once every hour. On Saturday and Sunday there is less frequent service, please check time table.

Travelling by car: If you want to rent a car it is advisable for visitors from abroad to negotiate the price at home before you come.
It takes 1 hour to drive from Frankfurt airport to Dornburg.
Follow signs A3 (Autobahn no.3) to Wiesbaden/ Cologne (Köln), exit Limburg Nord.
From Frankfurt City follow signs A66 Wiesbaden, A3 Cologne (Köln) 80km to Limburg, exit Limburg Nord towards B54 Siegen.
From Limburg: Road B54 to Siegen, exit Dornburg/Hadamar, turn left and go straight through Niederzeuzheim to Dornburg-Thalheim.
From Cologne (Köln): Autobahn A3 towards Frankfurt, 100km to Limburg, Exit Limburg Nord towards B54 Siegen.

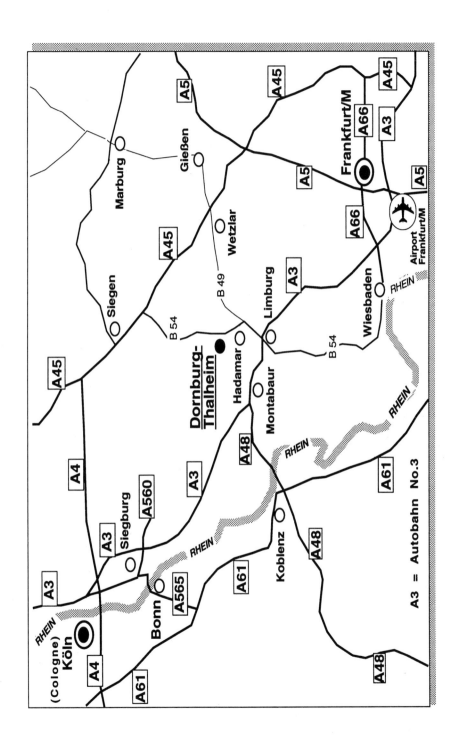

India 1979

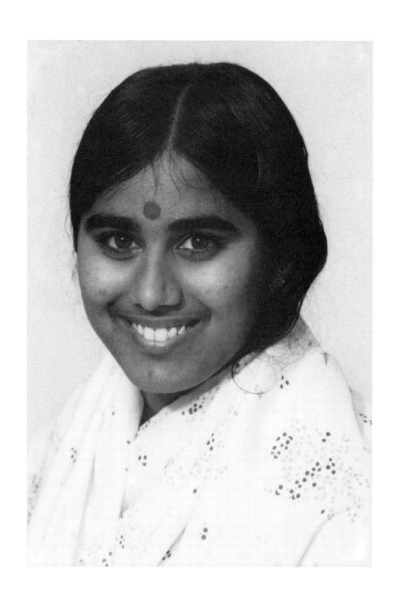

Essen, Germany 1981